MANCHESTER UNITED GREATS

Sir Matt Busby, President of Manchester United, on his recent 80th birthday, with the author.

MANCHESTER UNITED GREATS

DAVID MEEK

Foreword by
Sir Matt Busby

SPORTSPRINT PUBLISHING
EDINBURGH

Dedication

I would like to dedicate this book to the memory
of my late father, Wilf Meek,
who used to take me as a small boy on Sunday mornings
into the offices of the *Yorkshire Evening Press*
in Coney Street, York.
He would be taking in his report of the previous day's
York City game, a job he did for an incredible 45 years.
It was then that I wanted to become a journalist,
and now a lot of matches and books later
I am even more grateful
for the way he opened the window for me
into the world of newspapers and football.

John Donald Publishers Ltd.,
138 St. Stephen Street, Edinburgh EH3 5AA.

ISBN 0 85976 276 9

Phototypeset by Beecee Typesetting Services
Printed in Great Britain by Bell & Bain Ltd., Glasgow

Foreword

It seems many years ago since I wrote a foreword for David Meek's first book on Manchester United, but I recall then that I was pleased to do it because I have always felt that he had the interests of the club at heart.

A lot of football has been played in the intervening years and David has written a great many words about it, but I haven't changed my view about his integrity as a reporter or his ability to interest the reader.

I can't say I have agreed with everything he has written, but I do know that what he has said is because that is how he felt about it.

Now he draws on his long involvement with Old Trafford to tell us about the people who he feels are the ones to call the Greats of Manchester United.

I may well disagree with him again. I certainly don't envy him his task making the choice, but I look forward, as always, to what he has to say because I know it will revive many happy memories for me personally and perhaps for those of you who read the book.

Sir Matt Busby

Acknowledgements

I am indebted to Cliff Butler for his action photograph of Bryan Robson on the cover, and also to Harry Goodwin for his pictures along with the unfailing and cheerful assistance, as always, of Stan Royle, Picture Editor of my newspaper, the *Manchester Evening News.*

Even more importantly I must express my appreciation to Sir Matt Busby for his foreword and to the players, past and present, who by their presence on the great Manchester United stage have not only provided me with this book, but enabled me to enjoy my most pleasurable of jobs.

Contents

CHAPTER ONE

Introduction

Manchester United are probably better known for their players than their trophies!

The club have had their prize moments of course, but when conversation turns to Old Trafford it's more likely to be the famous names that are recalled rather than great victories or outstanding campaigns.

I have long believed that the cult of the personality and the entertainer has been one of the main ingredients contributing to the club's long reign as the best supported in the country.

It's been the brilliance of their performers that has prompted people like Bobby Charlton to perceive Old Trafford as a theatre of dreams.

The situation provides a fertile field for producing a book of this nature featuring the United Greats, though the very richness does also present considerable embarrassment when limiting the selection to ten.

So straightaway I offer my apologies to the many footballers of greatness who have been squeezed out of my team.

My starting point was not difficult because Sir Matt Busby is the father of the present-day Manchester United, and he was there at the start of the post-war era which for obvious reasons is the period I know best.

Indeed I have watched nearly all my chosen Greats in my capacity as the *Manchester Evening News* correspondent covering Manchester United since the Munich air crash in 1958. As a fan I saw the 1948 team and the Busby Babes.

So I studied the distinctive Johnny Carey who walked into great company because he was such an influential figure on the field as Busby and Jimmy Murphy set about their task of wakening the sleeping giant that was Manchester United.

Jack Rowley played in Busby's first team as well and was a phenomenal striker of the ball as reflected in his nickname of the Gunner. But I have got to say that he is also there as a representative because he played in a splendid side and there is no doubt that he wouldn't have reached the heights he did if it had not been for those around him like Stan Pearson, Johnny Morris, Charlie Mitten and indeed Jimmy Delaney, Matt's first player signing.

Duncan Edwards, the greatest of them all in many folk's esteem, must also stand for the Busby Babes, so many of them cut off hardly in their prime.

Roger Byrne, acknowledged as possibly the finest captain the club have had, along with players like Billy Whelan, Tommy Taylor and Eddie Colman, must let the incomparable Edwards speak for them.

I am on safer ground with the post-Munich team because no-one can deny the impact of that famous footballing litany of Charlton, Law and Best.

I shall still feel slightly guilty, though, when I next meet Dennis Viollet, still a record holder after scoring 32 League goals in season 1959-60. I don't know whether I shall be able to look Pat Crerand in the eye either after subscribing wholeheartedly to the notion in the Sixties that when Crerand plays well, United play well.

He might well wonder why his fellow team-mate Nobby Stiles is in ahead of him; but not many United players — only two in fact — have both a European Cup winner's medal AND a World Cup winner's medal.

That's special, and so is the gritty effort which every team needs to win things, as both Sir Matt and Sir Alf Ramsey acknowledged.

I have no hesitation either including Bryan Robson who at times seems to have carried both Manchester United and England on his shoulders. The mind boggles when you ponder what he would have been like in a really good team!

Hopefully we're about to find out under manager Alex Ferguson, and undoubtedly will do if my final great player, Mark Hughes, lives up to expectations.

The Welshman still has a little to prove, but he is there as one for the future, already fulfilling the prime requirement for a Manchester United player as one who excites and entertains and makes our football dreams just that little bit more real.

CHAPTER TWO

Sir Matt Busby

Sir Matt Busby, a legend in his own lifetime, is the architect of the Manchester United we know today.

Without him the famous Red Devils might still be just another football club, instead of an institution known all over the world.

Certainly between the two world wars there had been little to suggest that Old Trafford would grow to hold a special place in the hearts and minds of people who love the game of football.

Indeed the club was on its uppers when Matt arrived

Sir Matt Busby . . . President of Manchester United in familiar thoughtful mood.

home from the war in 1945 to be appointed to his first and last job in management.

Old Trafford was blitzed and out of action; the club was virtually bankrupt.

Yet from those unpromising beginnings, Busby was to build a club which took its place in the forefront of the game, and he kept it there for the whole of his 25-year reign as manager.

Others have followed to add even more sophisticated touches, so that today we see probably the finest club stadium in the land with a tradition for attracting the biggest crowds in the country.

But without the solid foundations laid by Busby over the years, there would have been nothing to build on. Manchester United might well have continued as a sleeping giant.

Matt roused the giant to become a trail blazer. He was a great innovator as he defied authority to lead English football into European competition as well as giving the game the acclaimed Busby Babes.

His resilience is unparalleled in football, recovering as he did from the calamity of the Munich air disaster to create more fine teams with players who became household names.

Yet his life started humbly enough. He was born on May 26th, 1909, in a two-roomed pitman's cottage in Orbiston, a small Lanarkshire mining village just outside Glasgow.

Life was probably a struggle. His father and all his uncles were killed in the first world war with the result that the remainder of the family started to emigrate to America in search of a better life than coal mining.

Matt's mother was due to join her sister while Matt waited for a visa to go as well. But then came one of those events which change the course of life.

He had been playing for one of his local teams, Denny Hibs, when out of the blue came an invitation to join Manchester City.

Matt's mother cancelled her plans for America and Matt

set out in 1928 with all the hope in the world to seek fame, if not fortune, in football at Maine Road.

There were times when I guess he must have wished he had gone to America because he struggled to make progress at City and at one point it looked as if he wouldn't make it.

Then came another of those sudden quirks of fate which prove to be so meaningful. He had been playing as an inside forward but because of injuries he was switched to play at wing half in the reserves, and it quickly became obvious that that was his position.

A regular place in the first team soon cured the homesick feeling and he prospered to become captain of the team, winning an F.A. Cup medal against Portsmouth in 1934 after losing in the final to Everton the previous year.

In 1936 Matt felt he wanted a change of club and he joined Liverpool where he played until the outbreak of war in 1939.

In common with most of the team he joined the army and served in the 9th Battalion of the King's Liverpool. Later he was transferred to the Army Physical Training Corps because of his sporting background.

At the end of the war Liverpool wanted him to resume playing and also become assistant manager to George Kay, but James Gibson, the chairman of Manchester United, had other ideas.

He had seen the qualities of management in Busby during his time at City and in an inspired moment offered him the post of full manager at United.

Walter Crickmer, the secretary, had acted as manager during the war following the departure of Scott Duncan, and Gibson had been on the lookout for the right man.

He could hardly have guessed at the success which lay ahead, but he was convinced Busby was the man for the job. He was the kind of man used to having his own way, but he yielded when the young Sergeant-Major insisted that he needed a five-year contract rather than the one for three years being offered.

Sir Matt outside his beloved Old Trafford and the club he served so well as manager for 25 years.

Busby had ideas, but he knew he had to have time to put them into effect . . . time to plant little acorns which would grow into strong oak trees, as Jimmy Murphy once described it.

Then he went out to become football's first track-suited manager. Before the war the typical manager spent most of his time in the office. The touchline was the nearest he got to the actual pitch.

In those days it was a revolutionary move. As Johnny Carey recalls: 'When I joined United, Scott Duncan, with spats and a red rose in his buttonhole, typified a soccer manager.

'But Matt Busby played with us in training, demonstrating what he wanted and it was quite new.'

The fresh approach made an immediate impact. When he took over as manager in October, 1945, United were 16th in the table; by the end of the season they had climbed to fourth.

United were launched and the following season, 1946-47, as football returned to a national basis instead of being divided into North and South, they finished League runners-up, just one point ironically behind Liverpool.

United finished second for two more seasons until Busby landed his first trophy, winning the F.A. Cup in 1948, by beating Blackpool in the final with the kind of expressive, entertaining football which was to carry the Busby stamp throughout his career.

Some critics reckon Busby inherited his first team, and it's true there were many fine players already on the books and coming home from the war like Stan Pearson, Jack Rowley, Charlie Mitten and Johnny Carey; but many a manager has taken over a good team and then proceeded to make nothing of it.

Busby underlined his talents by following up his Cup success with the League championship in 1952, four points in front of Spurs.

If that had been the end of the story one might have been tempted to think that Busby had been lucky with his first lot of players, but there was nothing accidental about the work he was busy accomplishing at the grass roots.

His scouts were out and about quietly bringing schoolboys to the club so that with the help of coaches like Bert Whalley he could fashion them into players in his own image.

Murphy, who was spotted by Busby giving a team talk to soldiers in Italy where he was in charge of a sports centre, had a special responsiblity for the youth team.

Matt Busby was a Sergeant-Major during the war and toured in Army teams to entertain the troops. Here in Naples he lines up in a star-studded side.
Back row: Jack Martin, Willie Watson, Tommy Lawton, Bert Sproston, Frank Swift, Danny Winter, Joe Mercer.
Front: Billy Elliott, Matt Busby, George Smith, Douglas Howe.

His little acorns first showed as sturdy young saplings who won the F.A. Youth Cup from its inception in 1952-53 for five seasons on the trot.

Soon they were challenging the old guard and one by one they took over until Matt took a team to Kilmarnock to play in a friendly and used most of his youngsters.

'I walked the golf course thinking that this was the time to go the whole way', he recalls. So in came Duncan Edwards, Dennis Viollet and Jackie Blanchflower to squeeze out three more veterans and the Busby Babes were born.

'From the very start I had envisaged making my own players, having a kind of nursery so that they could be trained in the kind of pattern I was trying to create for Manchester United,' he explains.

Busby was in fact a pioneer of a concentrated youth policy, and it paid him dividends. The club had always tried to encourage youngsters and during the war they had operated the Manchester United Junior Athletic Club.

This was really for local boys. Busby, man of vision, had a far wider outlook and began bringing the cream of schoolboys from much wider afield, especially from the two Irelands where he was well served by Bob Bishop in Belfast and Billy Behan in Dublin.

The value of his scheme, soon to become the blueprint for every major club, was borne out very quickly in the League championship.

His Babes took a couple of seasons to find their feet, and then there was no stopping them. They took the First Division by storm in season 1955-56, winning the title 11 points ahead of Blackpool with a team whose average age was little more than 21.

It wasn't meanness which drove Busby to produce his own players. It was their spirit and character he wanted to catch young so that once they wore the red shirt there was a pride and determination difficult to calculate in cash.

He was in fact free with United's money in the transfer market whenever he thought it necessary and there was a position to fill which couldn't be covered from within the club.

Right through his career he broke transfer records, starting with the weird fee of £29,999 for Barnsley centre forward Tommy Taylor when he realised he hadn't got a big bustling centre forward quite ready for promotion to the first team.

His fee of £45,000 for Albert Quixall was a record in its day, and so, too, was the £115,000 he paid Torino to bring Denis Law home from Italy.

He didn't blink when he created a record bid for a goalkeeper when he paid Chelsea £55,000 for Alex Stepney, and later said that the signing was the biggest single factor in winning the championship of 1967.

He was always willing to back his judgment with hard cash, and he was rarely wrong, but he gave his name to the Babes and they repaid him handsomely.

Busby built a strong management team which soon helped him to capture honours after the war. Proudly displaying some of his early trophies with him are Jimmy Murphy on the left, his invaluable assistant, and on the right, Bert Whalley, his much respected coach who died in the Munich air crash.

They followed up their runaway success in 1956 by winning the title the following year. They were champions by Easter and their 64 points total was the highest for 26 years.

They would have won the F.A. Cup that year as well but for losing goalkeeper Ray Wood with a broken cheekbone in the final against Aston Villa.

And all the time they were opening up new horizons in Europe contrary to the wishes of the insular Football League and Football Association.

Both bodies had tried to prevent United accepting an invitation to compete in the European Cup, but Matt, backed by his chairman was determined.

He explains: 'Football had become a world game and no longer belonged exclusively to the British Isles. I was eager to be part of the new European challenge.

'There was money to be made for the club, there was a

new excitement for the players and the opportunity for spectators to enjoy the skills of Continental players.

'It also seemed to me to be the logical progression, that the champions of England should pit their talents against the best of Europe. You can't make progress by standing still.'

Thus did Matt Busby demonstrate once again his visionary outlook, as well as going on to display the resolution to turn a dream into reality.

It took a few more years for the politicians with their European Common Market to follow down the same road!

Busby straightaway showed that back home he had a team ready for the challenge. England were failing in the fifties on the international stage, but Busby gave people the feeling that at least an English club could restore their shattered pride.

United scored some notable victories and reached the semi-finals at the first attempt.

Then everything came to an earth-shattering stop at Munich on February 6, 1958. It was a tragedy shared by millions round the world.

For Matt Busby the sense of loss must have been overpowering . . . his friends, his players, his staff, the newspaper men, so many killed and others who would never play again.

His immediate problem of course was his own fight for life; badly injured, he lay at death's door.

This was the time in his life when his true mettle showed through as he painfully dragged himself back to fitness. He was in agony for a year with his back after returning to work, but he never complained.

There was the weight of the responsibility as well. If he hadn't led his club into Europe there could have been no crash.

He says now: 'I need no reminding of the bitter sadness and suffering of Munich. I grieve still for those we lost. For a long while the responsibility of urging us down that road to Europe weighed heavily on my mind, but of course no-

Matt Busby almost captured a League and Cup double in 1957. His Busby Babes had won the League and expected to beat Aston Villa in the F.A. Cup. But as he leads his side out at Wembley Busby little thought he would lose his goalkeeper with a smashed cheekbone after a collision with Peter McParland.

one was to know the catastrophe that lay ahead. Like the rest of life we just have to do our best and do what seems right at the time.'

He agonised over whether to carry on in football. With the encouragement of his wife, Jean, he decided the club must continue and that he simply couldn't just walk away.

So he returned to accomplish what was perhaps an even greater achievement than his initial success . . . he simply built another great team.

Five years after the air crash he won the F.A. Cup and after another five he completed his life's work by making Manchester United the first English champions of Europe.

He gave us Bobby Charlton, Denis Law and George Best among a stream of talented players. His football philosophy was to win of course, but to try to do it with a certain style. He liked personalities out on the field and he gave them their head. They entertained and their manager was a powerful influence for the right kind of soccer for 25 years, through success and adversity.

He remained true to that ideal until he finally retired in 1971. He fashioned three quite separate teams of great distinction . . . the immediate post-war team which won the F.A. Cup in 1948, the Busby Babe side so cruelly destroyed in 1958 before it was in fact in full flower, and then the star-studded team which crowned his career by winning the European Cup in 1968.

In all Busby won the League championship on five occasions, he collected the F.A. Cup twice out of four finals, the F.A. Youth Cup six times and of course the European Cup, not to mention maintaining First Division status throughout his United career.

Considerable personal honours came his way. He was awarded the CBE in 1959, he was given the freedom of Manchester in 1967 and he was knighted the following year.

Pope Paul conferred on him in 1972 one of the highest civil decorations of the Roman Catholic Church when he made him a Knight Commander of St Gregory the Great.

It was a much appreciated honour, for while never ostentatious about his religion, Sir Matt has always been a man of faith. He is what I would call a quiet believer.

I believe he was also greatly pleased when his adopted city gave him its Freedom. He looked a proud man when he became Manchester sport's first Freeman, standing at the Town Hall with red carnation jaunty in his buttonhole, white tie and tails immaculate and the silver insignia of a Commander of the British Empire tucked snugly round his neck.

He chose that moment to reveal his deep love and feeling for football behind the honours and titles.

Manchester United were the first English club to win the European Cup thanks to Busby's determination to conquer fresh fields in face of opposition from the League and F.A.
Back row: Bill Foulkes, John Aston, Jimmy Rimmer, Alex Stepney, Alan Gowling, David Herd.
Middle: David Sadler, Freddie Owen (asst. secretary), Tony Dunne, Shay Brennan, Pat Crerand, George Best, Francis Burns, Joe Armstrong (chief scout), Jack Crompton (trainer).
Front: Jimmy Ryan, Nobby Stiles, Denis Law, Sir Matt Busby (manager), Bobby Charlton, Brian Kidd, John Fitzpatrick.

'I wouldn't deny that it is pleasant to succeed in what you strive to do,' he said.

'But winning matches at all costs is not the test of true achievement. There's nothing wrong with trying to win, as long as you don't set the garland and the prize above the game. There's no dishonour in defeat, as long as you play to the limit of your strength and skill.

'If the game isn't always played in that spirit, it's

unfortunate; and there have been incidents which have brought no credit to the game.

'I think it is well, therefore, that I should say that what matters above all things is that the game should be played in the right spirit, with the utmost resource of skill and courage, with fair play and no favour, with every man playing as a member of a team, and the result accepted without bitterness or conceit.

'Played at its best between first-class teams, football is a wonderful spectacle. I love its drama, its smooth playing skill, its long carefully laid rhythm, with the added flavour of sometimes contrasting styles.

'And its great occasions are for me at any rate unequalled in the world of sport. I feel a sense of romance, wonder and mystery, a sense of beauty and a sense of poetry.

'On such occasions the game is larger than life. It has something of the timeless magical quality of legend.'

Those words summed up the philosophy which lay behind his management and which he strove like the great teacher he was to instil into his players.

For there was much more to Matt Busby than knowledge of football, shrewd and far-seeing though that was. He was a good judge of a player, his character as well as his ability. But there are many such managers; Busby had more and was a natural leader.

His players respected him as a man as well as a manager. His authority was wielded with a quiet dignity. A summons to his office was like a visit to one's first headmaster. He attracted great loyalty; he could inspire confidence.

Ranting and raving was never his way. He had an avuncular air, and infinite patience, but he could be hard and even ruthless when he thought it was necessary.

Very early in his career he didn't hesitate to transfer Johnny Morris to Derby County for a then British record fee of £24,000. There was no question mark about the ability of a gifted inside forward who had been a key man in the 1948 Cup success, but he still had to go.

Sir Matt Busby and his wife, Jean, on the occasion he was made an honorary Freeman of Manchester in recognition of his services to the city.

He had questioned the authority of the manager and Busby wasn't going to have that. Jack Crompton, goal-keeper at the time and later the trainer at Old Trafford, told me: 'As a player at the time I thought the Boss was wrong because if Johnny Morris had stayed we would probably have won the Cup again.

'But later I knew he was right. You've got to have discipline and it was important in those early days for the Boss to establish his command. He must have been tempted to go for the soft option, but he didn't, and the incident served him well. It was what made him such an outstanding manager.'

Busby made a similar firm stand a few years later when Denis Law, one of the jewels in his team and in fact the apple of his eye, demanded more money and threatened a transfer request to try and get it.

Law was simply put on the list and told the tail doesn't

wag the dog at Manchester United; more to the point, a player doesn't tell Matt Busby what to do.

Denis didn't really want to leave and his bluff was called. Matt called a Press conference and peace was made, but only after Denis had stood in front of the television cameras to tell the world that he had made a mistake and had been badly advised.

Busby reigned supreme. He ran a tight ship, just another of the qualities which made him so successful for so long. What was so impressive was that he did it in such a composed, controlled way . . . as the player discovered who marched into his office one day to demand more money.

He didn't get it and by the end of the interview he was apologising and thanking him. It was only when he had got outside again that he thought what on earth am I thanking him for!

The way Busby exercised his authority was a great gift, like his incredible knack of remembering people's names. He never lost the common touch. In his time he mixed with the greatest and was quite at ease.

But he was just as comfortable with humble folk. He was never swept away by success. Until late in life he continued to live in the house in Chorlton-cum-Hardy where he had raised his family, Sandy and Sheena.

Always a big family man, he delights in his grand-children and is the first to tell you about his life's support from the late Lady Busby.

Jean died in December, 1988, after a long distressing illness that saw her unable to recognise her family. But she was visited every day by her husband with the kind of unfailing love and loyalty she had put into their marriage.

Jean helped enormously during the crisis of Munich, caring for distressed relatives, despite her own man's fight for life. Then she gave him the strength and inspiration to carry on in football.

Says Sir Matt now: 'I remember it all, every detail of it. It is always with me. The crash, the loss of the boys hit me so hard I didn't see how I could carry on.

'I thought I had done everything I could and that fate had intervened and destroyed everything.

'But a voice kept saying: "You cannot quit, you have to go on for the sake of the lads who died, for those coming through and for the people."

'It was the voice of my dear wife. She told me that Duncan Edwards and Roger Byrne would have wanted me to go on, that we had built something worth fighting for, whatever the odds.

'It took me some time to believe this but she was patient and persistent. She had her way and now as I look back I thank her for the last 31 years which have been such a bonus.'

Since the death of his wife, Sir Matt has taken to travelling more with the team again. He is welcomed everywhere he goes because he is held in great affection not just for what he achieved but for the way he did it.

Created the club's first President, Sir Matt celebrated his 80th birthday on May 26, 1989, truly the grand old man of English football who will be remembered for all time as the father of the modern-day Manchester United.

CHAPTER THREE

Johnny Carey

Johnny Carey was possibly the last of the great Corinthians in professional soccer, certainly at Manchester United, the club he graced for 17 years.

He was always known as 'Gentleman John', easy-going, pipe-smoking and quite imperturbable. Nothing ever seemed to bother him, either on or off the field.

It's easy to see him like that now of course as he heads for his 70th birthday, a genial man who inevitably graduated to golf as a natural expression for a sportsman who was always so cool, calm and collected.

But those who knew him as a player say he was exactly the same.

John Doherty, the former United player, who moved on to Leicester before knee injury ended his skilful playing days, made his debut when Carey was the captain.

'I can't recollect him every getting annoyed, not even if someone had kicked him. He seemed to stroll through games. If he was playing today he would be called laid back. Then we just thought he was unflappable.

'The great thing of course was that he was a great player and as a captain his influence was immense. He was a thinker, but not a shouter,' recalls Doherty.

Indeed not, and perhaps Carey was helped as a great captain because he captained a great side. Carey's era just after the war saw players returning from the services, mature men who knew a real leader by experience.

They didn't have to be hollered at, and in that sense Johnny Carey was in the right place at the right time.

He arrived at Old Trafford in 1936 almost by accident,

Johnny Carey, Manchester United's great post-war captain, when he was manager of Nottingham Forest after taking them to second place behind United in the 1967 League championship.

spotted by Louis Rocca, United's chief scout associated with the club for an incredible 55 years.

Rocca tells the story of his signing: 'I was sent over to Dublin to sign a player from Bohemians named Gaughan. Scott Duncan, our manager at that time, told me that everything had been fixed for the lad to join us.

'My job was simple — so it seemed. Just to get him to sign the necessary forms and bring him back with me to Old Trafford.

'I contacted Gaughan all right, only to learn of some hidden snag. It appeared that Glasgow Celtic wanted him, and as a Scottish club could pay a player any fee they liked, Gaughan naturally enough decided to hang on.

'He eventually signed for them and received £400. I had

spent the best part of a week trying to get him to change his mind, but on the Friday evening he became a Celtic player. Later he went to Southampton and Sunderland.

'I was upset about the whole thing, but decided to stay over the weekend and on the Sunday I went along to see St. James's Gate, then an unknown team to me. It was a poor game, but . . .

'There was something about the inside right which took my fancy. In a short time I was satisfied he would make the grade, asked his name and after the match went straight to the club secretary and told him of my mission.

'A meeting of the committee was called there and then. We talked for hours and eventually I got Carey's signature for £200.

'I went to see Johnny's father before Johnny decided to come to England. His consent was readily given, and Mr Carey gave me a real homely Irish welcome which lasted until the early hours of the next morning.

'Next day young Johnny came to England with me. When we reached Manchester he noticed a newspaper bill which said: "United sign star."

'Johnny looked at me and we bought a paper. It told us that Thompson had signed for Manchester United from Blackburn. Then right at the end was a two-line paragraph about Johnny Carey's signing.

'Neither of us said anything.'

That was the embarrassing and inauspicious arrival in Manchester of the young Carey.

I imagine neither of them had any real notion that this was a 17-year-old player who would become a giant among giants, a man who was so versatile that he figured in nine different positions for United, ten if you include the occasion he pulled on the goalkeeper's jersey when Jack Crompton was taken ill at an away match.

Rocca later declared: 'No greater Irish player crossed the Channel to make a name in English football, and yes, I can recall stars like Billy Gillespie, Elisha Scott, Peter Doherty and Micky Hamill.'

On the strength of service in the British Army, Carey was granted the unusual distinction of playing for both his native Republic of Ireland and Northern Ireland.

Carey became Matt Busby's on-field lieutenant, a captain who was a perfect extension of his manager's philosophy. He led his team to honours, he was voted

Footballer of the Year by the soccer writers and he was fêted in the boardroom when he retired.

He became a distinguished international with the unusual distinction of playing for both the Republic of Ireland and Northern Ireland. In 1947 he captained the Rest of Europe against Great Britain.

But all that was still to come. First Carey had to make his way at Old Trafford. Scott Duncan gave him his debut early in season 1937-38 in a home match against Southampton.

He played in the next game at inside right, but both were defeats and he lost his place. He returned at inside left just after Christmas and this time the results were better and he shared in an unbeaten run which helped United finish Second Division runners-up.

The following season he helped United consolidate in the First Division with 32 appearances and six goals to claim a respectable 14th place.

Then of course came the war and as a neutral from Eire the youthful Carey could have gone back home, but he not only stayed, he joined up to serve in the Queen's Royal Hussars.

As Carey was to say later: 'A country which gives me my living is worth fighting for.'

It was a gesture which was to prove a long one, yet I doubt whether he ever questioned his decision; he was that kind of man, and it was just one of the things which endeared him to Manchester's sporting public.

Carey continued to play for United in wartime football until posted abroad to North Africa and Italy. He was away for two years and recalls: 'I landed in Algiers, the first of many calling places in the Middle East which eventually took me to Trieste in Northern Italy.'

While he was there he played for some of the local Italian teams, appearing in the programme as 'Cario'. In his unit was a young winger, also destined for great things, by name of Tom Finney.

'It was great fun. I had the job as a Sergeant to coach and

Manchester United's first championship after the war and a personal triumph for the leadership of the captain, Johnny Carey, and his manager Matt Busby, in 1952.

train all the football-minded personnel in the unit. It was good to go back to England, though, and link up with Manchester United again who had new players like Jack Crompton, Henry Cockburn and Joe Walton,' recalled Cario!

The other soldiers came back one by one as well at the end of the war, players like Jack Rowley, Stan Pearson, Charlie Mitten and John Aston. They met their new manager, Matt Busby, like themselves home from the war, and he quickly licked them into shape.

Busby was well off for forwards and he converted Carey to full back, no doubt softening the blow by making him the captain. Not that Carey would have objected. Nothing ruffled him and he took to his new position like a duck to water as United romped home to finish League runners-up in 1946-47, the first full competition following the war.

At the end of the season in May came the invitation to skipper the Rest of the World in a match to mark the re-entry of the English Football Association into FIFA.

The game was scheduled for Hampden Park in May, 1947, with a full-scale practice game arranged for the European team in a friendly against Holland.

Says Carey: 'I flew to Amsterdam to meet up with the rest of the players. It was a strange experience. Almost everybody spoke a different language and in terms of teamwork and understanding we were just like a Showbiz celebrity eleven.

'But we had a few good players and we beat the Dutch 2-1 which gave us high hopes of beating Great Britain.

'We went to Scotland and stayed at the Marine Hotel in Troon. I shall always remember it because one of the waitresses complimented me on my command of the English language! I suppose I was rather the odd one out among those Europeans.'

The game at Hampden was watched by 140,000 and there was no holding the British attack made up of Stan Matthews, Wilf Mannion, Tommy Lawton, Billy Steel and Billy Liddell.

They put six goals past Carey and the luckless French goalkeeper Daroi. 'It was no contest,' laughs Carey. 'Our team were like the strangers we were while the Great Britain boys knew exactly what they were doing. Still it was a great experience and a great honour to captain the Rest of Europe team.'

Back home United were continuing to impress and were responding to the leadership of Busby off the field and to Carey on it. 'We lacked consistency, but when we clicked there was no team in the country which could live with us,' was the captain's verdict.

Finishing second three years on the trot wasn't bad for consistency, though! And in the F.A. Cup they really made their mark, beating Blackpool in the 1948 final with a remarkable performance.

In the League they fell to fourth in season 1949-50, but quickly pulled themselves back on course to finish second again before finally exploding into championship form to give Carey the opportunity of holding the League trophy aloft.

It was midway through the 1951-52 title season that Carey underwent another of those dramatic changes of position which served the team so well.

Tommy McNulty was brought in at right back and Carey was switched to right half; and what a smooth, majestic figure he cut. Busby made his inspired alteration at the beginning of the December and United lost only twice between then and the end of the season.

Carey played in 38 games and scored three goals. It was Busby's first championship, indeed United's first since their early days in 1911.

Carey played on for one more season and then retired, his place at right half taken by one of the first Busby Babes to come through, Jeff Whitefoot. In football's notoriously small world, Whitefoot would later play for Carey at Nottingham Forest.

In all Johnny Carey made 306 League appearances for United and scored 17 goals. It would undoubtedly have been many more had the war not robbed him of six years' League football.

He played 36 times for the Republic of Ireland including a memorable 2-0 victory over England at Goodison Park in 1949. He was just as versatile on the international stage, appearing in seven different positions for his country to match his 10 for United.

He was certainly a man whose actions spoke louder than words, achieving his legendary reputation as a captain without, as one contemporary put it, 'saying a dicky bird.'

Like Busby his manager he had an aura of dignity which spoke for itself. Certainly his contribution to the 1952 championship helped to inspire a glowing tribute from the *Manchester Guardian* who accorded the team the unusual honour of granting them mention in their esteemed leader column.

The *Guardian* clearly saw the success as a triumph for the partnership of manager and captain. The leader writer eulogised: 'After an interval of 41 years, Manchester United have regained the championship of the Football League. The title has never been better earned.

'Not only has the team, in the five seasons before this one, finished second four times and fourth once in the League and won the F.A. Cup; it has been captained, managed and directed in a way that is a lesson to many others.

'J. Carey, the captain in this period, has been a model footballer — technically efficient thanks to hard work; a fighter to the last, without ever forgetting that he is a sportsman; a steadier of the younger and inexperienced, and inspirer of the older and tiring, and at all times the most modest of men, though he has won every football honour open to him.

'M. Busby, the manager, has shown himself as great a coach as he was a player, with an uncannily brilliant eye for young local players' possibilities, whether in their usual or in other positions; a believer in the certainty of good football's eventual reward, and a kindly, yet, when necessary, firm father of his family of players.

'Between them they have built up a club spirit which is too rare in these days, a spirit which enables men to bear cheerfully personal and team disappointments and to ignore personal opportunities to shine for the good of the whole.'

United themselves knew they had been given exceptional service by their model player, and when the moment came for his retirement in 1953 the directors took the unusual step of inviting Carey to their boardroom in order to express their appreciation.

The club minutes record: 'The directors expressed their deepest regret at his decision to end his playing career and unanimously agreed to put on record their great appreciation of his long and loyal service. By his outstanding personality as a true sportsman, the honours he had won

Johnny Carey with the ball at his feet as the captain lines up with Matt Busby's first squad.
Back row: Matt Busby (manager), Ronnie Burke, Jack Warner, Allenby Chilton, Jack Crompton, John Aston, Charlie Mitten, Billy McGlen, Tom Curry (trainer).
Front: Johnny Morris, Jimmy Delaney, Johnny Hanlon, Johnny Carey, Stan Pearson, Jack Rowley, Walter Crickmer (secretary).
Insets: John Anderson, Henry Cockburn.

as an international in club matches, he had covered his career with glory and set a shining example to all who follow him.'

Geoffrey Green, football correspondent of *The Times,* now retired and a contemporary of Carey's, clearly warmed to the man and brilliantly captured the magnificence of his play when he wrote in his official history of Manchester United:

'Here, indeed, was a man who had been one of the outstanding footballers of his time, an architect of constructive defence and almost as great in his ways as Matthews, the destroyer of defence. At first glance, with his thinning hair and thoughtful expression, he looked older than his true age. But there was no doubting his maturity. From the moment he led out his side, you got the impression that he was bringing out a pack of schoolboys who were to be put through their paces under his supervision.

'Not that he was overbearing. On the contrary. Yet there was something in his measured, stately tread that engendered an instant feeling of respect and authority. But Carey never encouraged any exploitation of his personality. For him the game was one thing; personal triumphs at best were an irrelevancy.

'Many other memories remain of Carey, the artist. His exact anticipation; the smooth unhurried positional play that carried him to the right place at the right moment with no more show than if he were taking a quiet stroll on a summer's evening; his exquisite balance and control, especially on a "sticky dog"; the way he measured his clearances, with the ball always used to the best advantage of the colleagues in front of him.

'And if sometimes he broke the accepted canons of a full back by beating his opponent in the dribble near the danger zone, well, never mind, it was something that could be excused in him, because he was above the lesser mortals.

'For, in effect, he was a full back who combined the constructive ability of wing half with the footwork and intelligence of an inside forward, and as such he mastered the arts and graces of the game.

'Carey, always the most generous of men and of opponents, had earned his plaudits to the end.'

When the captain decided to retire, United were keen to keep him on the staff. It was obvious that the qualities which had made him a great player would be a good influence in management and the directors offered him a post as a coach.

But Blackburn Rovers had also spotted the potential and made him a better offer as coach with more prospects of becoming a full manager. So, perhaps with some misgivings, off he went to Ewood Park with the best wishes of everyone connected with United.

It was the start of a new phase which was to bring him mixed fortunes and would certainly extend him after taking his playing career in something of a stroll.

A parade of the old guard being interviewed by the author. Left to right: Johnny Carey, Jack Rowley, Stan Pearson, Sir Matt Busby, Les Olive (secretary) and David Meek.

'Matt said he would find me a position at Old Trafford but said I had the necessary qualifications to become a successful manager and urged me to try my luck,' recalls Carey.

Things went well at Blackburn with the new man bringing the club into the First Division, a success which caught the attention of Everton.

He announced at the time: 'I've accepted the post of manager of Everton because it's a challenge I feel must be met. If I hadn't taken it, it's likely that all the rest of my life I'd have wondered just how I would have gone on and how I'd have tackled the job of raising the team to its one-time greatness.'

Barely three years later came one of the most bizarre sackings in a game which thinks nothing of axeing a man on Christmas Eve.

Everton chairman John Moores sacked Carey in a London taxi as the two of them left a meeting of League clubs at the Cafe Royal where ironically they had been discussing players' wages and contracts!

Carey was given 24 hours' notice and had two and a half years of his contract to run. Not unnaturally he went to law to seek proper recompense. When he took over, Everton were at the foot of the First Division table. He raised them to 16th and they finished 15th the following season.

When he was sacked he had them running second for a spell and in fact they finished fifth. But Mr Moores had not liked a run of eight defeats which had ended their actual title challenge and he had his eye on Harry Catterick, a former Everton player, who steered Sheffield Wednesday to a runners-up position.

But it remains a ruthless dismissal in the eyes of many followers of the game and Sir Matt Busby was among those disgusted at the cavalier treatment of his one-time captain.

But the man hadn't been deterred, and after a short break he was appointed manager of Leyton Orient and brought them out of the Second Division in second place behind Liverpool.

His philosophy was: 'I just keep on telling them to play football — and play it on the ground. Definitely no strong-arm stuff.'

There were certainly echoes of his old mentor and manager there, though the fairy story ended abruptly with relegation back to the Second Division the following season.

But his purist approach to the way football should be played found a sympathetic ear at Nottingham Forest and for five years between 1963 and 1968 'Gentleman Johnny' found a good spiritual home at the City Ground.

His team talks were based on the simple instruction to 'fizz it about', though he did concede at one point: 'To survive these days you have got to have the killer instinct. You've got to have players with the hardness and drive that wins matches.'

To help him in this department he recruited the more outgoing Tommy Cavanagh, a trainer who knew all about cracking the whip, and together they produced a class side which in season 1966-67 finished second in the First Division.

Ahead of them as champions were Manchester United, master and one-time pupil heading the field. Matt Busby must have felt good that year.

Keeping Forest in the big-time proved difficult and after half a season without a home win in 1968 he was asked to leave. Blackburn Rovers stepped in again to make him their administrative manager and so complete a 16-year circle.

After 18 months he swopped places with Eddie Quigley to take charge of the team, but couldn't prevent relegation to the Third Division, for the first time in the club's history.

That summer proved the end of the management road for Johnny at Ewood Park, and everywhere else for that matter. Typically he went with his philosophy still intact. 'It's all part of the job', he said.

He had had his moments as a manager, though he hadn't quite matched the peerless achievements of his playing career, but then that was always going to be a well-nigh impossible task.

He was content after that to take a job in the Borough Treasurer's office at Sale, Cheshire, a far cry from football life, but he was never a man with any pretensions.

United and Tommy Docherty brought him out of retirement for a spell to do some part-time scouting, but golf took over from football to fill his sporting interests. He is a keen and able golfer at Bramhall Park, Cheshire, and says: 'Saturdays are given over to the golf now, but I still think football is a terrific game.

'I perhaps wish people would accept defeat with a little more grace and I would like to see the players allowed to express themselves more.

'But soccer is super, the best game in the world.'

JOHNNY CAREY'S RECORD

	LEAGUE		F.A. CUP		TOTAL	
	App	Gls	App	Gls	App	Gls
1937-38	16	3	3	1	19	4
1938-39	32	6	2		34	6
1939-40	2	1			2	1
1945-46			4		4	
1946-47	31		2		33	
1947-48	37	1	6		43	1
1948-49	41	1	7		48	1
1949-50	38	1	5		43	1
1950-51	39		4		43	
1951-52	38	3	1		39	3
1952-53	32	1	4		36	1
	306	17	38	1	344	18

REPUBLIC OF IRELAND: 1937 v Norway; 1938 v Czechoslovakia, Poland, Switzerland, Poland; 1939 v Hungary (twice), Germany; 1946 v Portugal, Spain, England; 1947 v Spain, Portugal; 1948 v Portugal, Spain, Switzerland; 1949 v Belgium, Portugal, Sweden, Spain, Finland, England, Finland, Sweden; 1950 v Norway; 1951 v Argentina, Norway; 1952 v France; 1953 v Austria (29 caps).

NORTHERN IRELAND: 1946 v England, Scotland; 1947 v Wales, England; 1948 v England, Scotland; 1949 v Wales (7 caps).

REST OF EUROPE: 1947 v Great Britain.

CHAPTER FOUR

Jack Rowley

They didn't call Jack Rowley 'The Gunner' for nothing as Manchester United blazed into prominence just after the last war.

Scoring goals was the name of the game for this traditionally orthodox centre forward from the Black Country who became a big favourite with the fans who loved his blockbusting shots and cannon headers.

Jack is one of the all-time scoring greats for Manchester United and many think he should have won more than his six caps for England.

Unfortunately he played in an era of Tommy Lawton and Nat Lofthouse who between them dominated the international stage with Tom Finney and Stanley Matthews blocking the wing positions where he also played with great success for United.

But his absence from the England team takes nothing away from his scoring feats for his club. He scored 208 goals in 422 League and F.A. Cup appearances, which is a remarkable record when you consider that the Army took six and a half years out of his playing career.

Not that he stopped scoring during the war when he guested for Spurs, Wolves and Irish club Distillery among other clubs, and it's war-time football which provides him with one of his most cherished memories.

He recalls: 'I played for Spurs one week and scored seven goals, and then a few days later I got eight out of eight for Wolves.'

He dominated United's scoring in the post-war years, especially on the big occasions. He hit two in the F.A. Cup final victory over Blackpool in 1948, and he broke the club's scoring record in season 1951-52 to help win the League championship.

His shot was reckoned to be the hardest of his day, a finish in keeping with his strong, aggressive style which was always a feature of his game.

Perhaps that's why if he's watching a game these days it is likely to be on the touchline of his local Rugby Union club rather than Old Trafford.

And if he is not just down the road from his home in Shaw, Oldham, he's probably a guest at Swinton Rugby League Club and enjoying it.

'I'm still interested in soccer, but it's convenient to watch the rugby three minutes away. I also like the way they take the knocks, shake them off and then later are the best of pals in the bar,' he explained.

'I was always hard but fair as a player and I see that kind of attitude more in rugby these days than I do in soccer,' he added.

Jack was born in Wolverhampton to a footballing family. His father was a goalkeeper with Walsall who even played at inside forward for a local team when he was nearly 60. His three sons all played. Albert the eldest had his career cut short by injury. Arthur the youngest played for Leicester and became a legendary scoring stalwart for Shrewsbury Town where he set all kinds of records including 38 goals in the Third Division in season 1958-59.

Jack started out as an outside left and soon after leaving school became part of Major Frank Buckley's famous nursery at Wolves as a ground staff boy. He was loaned out to Cradley Heath in the Birmingham League.

United's scouts were keeping tabs on him by now, but Wolves clearly didn't rate him all that highly because they let him move on to Bournemouth.

When he scored 10 League goals in 11 games at Dean Court United manager Scott Duncan moved in quickly and bought him for £3,000. He had only been at the south coast club for five months.

He played his first game for United against Sheffield

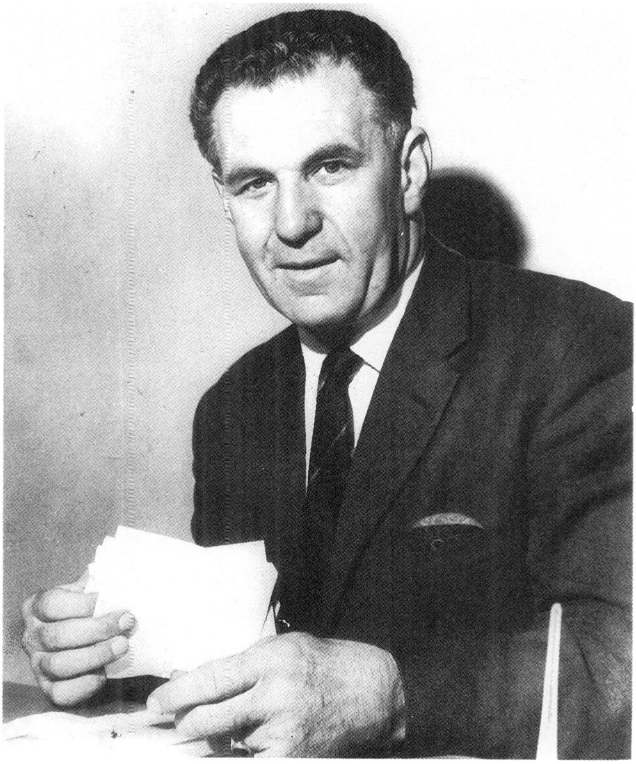

Jack Rowley, whose managerial career covered Plymouth Argyle, Oldham Athletic, Ajax of Amsterdam, Wrexham, Bradford and Oldham again.

Wednesday on October 23, 1937, at Old Trafford, playing on the left wing and sharing in a 1-0 win.

He felt out of it, though, and asked to be played in the reserves in order to get used to his new surroundings. His modesty paid off handsomely because when he was brought back a month later into the first team he scored four goals in a 5-1 win against Swansea.

There was no looking back and he stayed in the side, missing only one match through injury, to score nine goals in 25 appearances, good going for an 18-year-old winger.

His goals helped the Reds finish runners-up in the Second Division to go straight back to the top grade. There remained just one more season before the outbreak of war with Rowley bagging a useful 10 goals from 38 games, still playing at outside left.

Like many of his team-mates he joined up and served with the South Staffordshire Infantry. He was an anti-tank gunner and took part in the Normandy landings in France.

After the war he returned to take his place in what became the all-star forward line which featured himself at centre forward flanked by Stan Pearson and Johnny Morris with Jimmy Delaney and Charlie Mitten on the wings.

It took a season, though, before the famous five settled into that formation. The first season after the war saw Rowley playing half the season on the wing while new manager Matt Busby juggled around with other players like Jack Burke and Johnny Hanlon.

But there was no doubting that Gunner Rowley was back in the shooting business as he rattled in 26 League goals from 37 appearances for the Reds to finish championship runners-up.

Season 1947-48 saw United again League runners-up with a similar goal contribution from Rowley of 23 from 39 appearances, nearly all at centre forward now. But of course it was in the F.A. Cup that United made the football world sit up and take notice, and confirm the arrival of their all-star attack.

They overwhelmed the opposition in every round. They didn't need any replays and scored 22 goals in six games, including of course four in their highly entertaining victory over Blackpool in the final at Wembley. Rowley contributed five goals in the Cup run, two of them in the final.

They opened with a scoring spectacular to win 6-4 at Villa Park in the third round. Villa made the mistake of scoring first because it stung their opponents into avenging action which saw them leading 5-1 at half time, with Rowley among the scorers.

The 1948 team were well known for slipping into freewheel when they felt they had done enough, and typically they let Villa back in to narrow the score to 5-4.

Jack Rowley as The Gunner, famous for his goals at Old Trafford.

But, suitably alarmed, they moved back into gear for Stan Pearson to snuff out the revival and give the Reds their 6-4 victory.

Rowley was on target again in the fourth round against Liverpool which was a home tie that had to be played at Goodison Park because Old Trafford was out of action through war damage. A 74,000 crowd saw United win 3-0. Charlton were beaten 2-0 in the fifth round, this time the home tie being played on the Huddersfield ground.

The sixth round was in the slightly more familiar surroundings of Maine Road where United were playing all their home League games, and Rowley celebrated by scoring to lead the Manchester men to a 4-1 win.

The semi-final, played at Hillsborough, belonged to Stan Pearson, Rowley's scoring partner, who bagged a hat-trick to win 3-0 against a Derby County team which included great players like Carter, Stamps and Steel.

There were star names ranged against them when they came out for the final against Blackpool, not least the two Stans, Matthews and Mortensen. Blackpool were the first to score as well. Allenby Chilton brought down Mortensen who tumbled into the penalty area for Eddie Shimwell to give the Seasiders a 12th-minute lead. Jack Rowley got the all-important equaliser in the 28th minute when Jimmy Delaney's cross caught goalkeeper Joe Robinson and Eric Hayward in two minds.

Jack remembers: 'The ball came through and the two Blackpool players both called for it. I nipped between them as the goalkeeper went to collect it and stuck out my foot.

'Luckily for me, it connected. The ball went high in the air. I went round Robinson and then seemed to wait hours for the ball to come down. Eventually it did and I just had to side-foot it into the net.'

As a football reporter wrote at the time: 'It sounds easy, but only Jack Rowley would have been so nonchalant about it.'

Blackpool were full of fight, though, and only seven minutes later Mortensen shot them in front again. Once more The Gunner raced to the rescue!

Kelly handled and a quick free kick by Johnny Morris saw Rowley burst past Hayward to head powerfully into the roof of the net, a typical Gunner goal. There were 20 minutes left as the game mounted to the kind of climax that marked it out as one of the all-time great Cup finals, remarkable for not just its drama but the quality of the football.

The issue was tipped United's way in a twinkling movement which flowed from one end of the field to the other. Ten minutes from time Mortensen broke clear for Blackpool and hammered a tremendous shot towards the right-hand corner of goal.

Rowley in scoring action here against Blackpool at Old Trafford in Manchester United's championship season of 1951-52. Left to right: Stan Pearson, Rowley, Johnny Downie and Blackpool goalkeeper George Farm. Rowley's goal helped United to a 3-1 win and took the player another step nearer his record club tally of 30 that season.

Jack Crompton not only got to the shot, but held it and like a flash transferred the ball to the opposite end. He cleared with a big kick which was touched on by John Anderson for Stan Pearson to score with a fierce low shot from 25 yards which went in off the post to give Robinson no chance.

At the United end, Mortensen had still not got out of United's penalty area! Blackpool had been within an ace of leading for a third time and now they were behind.

United clinched the match when Anderson tried a speculative lob which caught Kelly's head and curled gently into his own net with Robinson hopelessly wrong-footed.

Rowley and company had brought the F.A. Cup to Manchester United after an absence of 39 years, and had become the first ever team to land the trophy after twice coming from behind.

Their winning line-up was:

Crompton, Carey, Aston, Anderson, Chilton, Cockburn, Delaney, Morris, Rowley, Pearson, Mitten.

Rowley was of course fortunate to play in front of such a commanding defence and half-back line, and as a centre forward he undoubtedly owed a great deal to his fellow forwards.

It was a magical attack without a weak link. Jimmy Delaney, Matt Busby's first signing at £5,000 from Glasgow Celtic, was a speedy right winger. Charlie Mitten, a local boy who had joined straight from school in 1936, was an equally quick raider on the left wing and is generally reckoned to have had the sweetest left peg in football. Johnny Morris, another young local recruit and later to play for Derby, was the schemer with great dribbling skill. Stan Pearson from Salford had played, like Rowley, before the war and also lost six years' prime playing time. He was the inside left who combined creative play with a splendid eye for goal. He and Rowley, in modern terms, were the strikers, and like his partner he returned outstanding figures.

Pearson scored 128 League goals in 315 League appearances for United as well as hitting 21 goals in 30 F.A. Cup ties. He had great rapport with Rowley, as he explains: 'For two or three seasons our forward line picked itself.

'We all got to know each other so well and instinctively we knew what was going to happen next. For instance, if Johnny Aston had the ball at left back I would come towards him, and I knew without looking that if I slipped it straight, Jack Rowley would be moving for it.

'He would then push it out to Charlie Mitten on the left wing and in seconds we had the ball in front of goal.

'They talk about one-touch football these days as if it's something new, but we were doing it in 1948, and in my view no team has done it better.'

The season after the F.A. Cup success was another good one for Rowley who maintained his career average of a goal every two games by notching 20 in 39 appearances to help the Reds finish League runners-up again.

Season 1949-50 saw The Gunner produce exactly the

The Gunner comes racing in but is beaten this time by Hanson in the Bolton goal.

same figures, though this time the team slipped slightly to fourth. The following year United were back to second in the table with 14 goals for Rowley, possibly down a bit because in the second half of the season he moved back to outside left with John Aston at centre forward.

But in season 1951-52 Manchester United had Jack Rowley back at centre forward and he duly responded by scoring a hat-trick in each of the first two games.

Indeed after only seven games he had rattled in an incredible 14 goals to set the scene for Busby's first championship triumph and the club's first for 41 years.

The team was getting a bit long in the tooth but the old

boys still had a shot left in their locker. Pearson scored 22 goals, but not to be outdone, Rowley improved his own club scoring record with 30 from 40 appearances.

Joe Spence had set a record in season 1927-28 when he had scored 22 League goals. Rowley took over with 26 in the first season after the war and now he had broken his own record which was to stand for another eight years until Dennis Viollet came along with 32.

The Rowley-inspired start to the title race slowed a little to leave Portsmouth the pace-setter, but they fell away to leave United, Spurs and Arsenal looking the chief challengers.

They were neck and neck on the final lap with the title actually decided by the very last game in a grand finale between United and Arsenal who had hit top form after Christmas.

Thanks to the high scoring of Rowley and Pearson, United had a much better goal average; so much so that Arsenal needed to win 7-0 to become champions, a tall order against United who in fact hammered home their superiority by spiking the Gunners 6-1.

What a way to finish, and of course it was The Gunner out-gunning the Gunners who showed the way by scoring a hat-trick, his fourth of the season. Jack had signed off the way he had started, and United took the title with 57 points to leave Spurs and Arsenal level on points four behind.

The team which clinched the championship read at the end of the season:

Allen, McNulty, Aston, Carey, Chilton, Cockburn, Berry, Downie, Rowley, Pearson, Byrne.

A few of the 1948 team like Jack Crompton, Jimmy Delaney, Johnny Morris and Charlie Mitten had faded from the scene for one reason or another, and others would follow.

But Jack Rowley had stamina, like Allenby Chilton, and the pair of them played for another three seasons until they were finally squeezed out by the brilliant Busby Babes.

They bridged the gap, though. Jack eventually lost his centre forward spot to Tommy Taylor, the boy from Barnsley destined to play for England, and he finally had to give way on the left wing to the youthful thrust of David Pegg and Albert Scanlon.

He scored goals right to the end, though, even if there weren't quite as many hat-tricks. His last game was on January 22, 1955, in a 1-1 draw with Bolton at Old Trafford.

His career with United had spanned 18 years, and not unnaturally he was granted a free transfer at the end of the season so that he could join Plymouth Argyle as player-manager. He played for a couple more years and then concentrated on management to take Argyle into the Second Division in 1959.

Football being the game it is, he was sacked six months later. It's also got to be said that Jack's management style was a bit like his play . . . aggressive and blunt. It didn't suit everyone, as became very evident in his next job as manager of Oldham Athletic. In three years at Boundary Park he lifted the average attendance from 4,000 to 15,000 and took them up to the Third Division.

But at the very moment of promotion triumph he was sacked after a cloak and dagger campaign by a split board of directors. He admitted at the time: 'Some seem to think I'm too tough a boss. Well, I call a spade a spade and do some straight talking.'

But even Oldham's elderly chairman, Frank Armitage, confessed about the sacking: 'It is disgusting that the manager of a club which has been lifted so high in the division should be sacked. This man has done wonderful things for the club. I am too disgusted for words.'

So Jack Rowley was out on his ear, though not for long. The Gunner became one of the early English managers to be head-hunted by a European club, long before it became fashionable for the likes of Terry Venables in Barcelona. Ajax took him to Amsterdam that summer on a two-year contract to succeed Vic Buckingham.

Again he was successful, taking the club to runners-up position in the Dutch League. Unfortunately a change of President and more internal politics meant that his contract wasn't renewed, so back to England he came for spells with Wrexham and Bradford.

Then in 1968 came a second call from Oldham who wanted Rowley to perform another miracle and keep them in the Third Division where he had taken them in his previous reign as manager. It was a move which suited him because during his first spell in Oldham he had put down roots and taken a Post Office and newsagent's shop in nearby Shaw.

'I have some unfinished business at Boundary Park,' said Jack. 'I hate leaving loose ends. All the people involved before have gone. I don't have any bad feelings about that.'

This time, though, the magic didn't work. Oldham went down and at Christmas the following season, they were knocked out of the F.A. Cup by a non-League team and were only two points above the bottom club.

Inevitably the axe fell and the curtain came down on Jack's managerial career. It was a sad, unsuccessful moment, but he had had plenty of happy memories and glory to look back on in his career.

'I enjoyed it all, playing and managing, but all good things come to an end,' says Jack, now retired from business as well as football as he heads for his 70th birthday. He and his wife still live in the area with three children and six grandchildren not far away from his adopted home.

JACK ROWLEY'S RECORD

	LEAGUE		F.A. CUP		TOTAL	
	App	Gls	App	Gls	App	Gls
1937-38	25	9	4	—	29	9
1938-39	38	10	1	—	39	10
1945-46	—	—	4	2	4	2
1946-47	37	26	2	2	39	28
1947-48	39	23	6	5	45	28
1948-49	39	20	8	9	47	29
1949-50	39	20	5	3	44	23
1950-51	39	14	3	1	42	15
1951-52	40	30	1	—	41	30
1952-53	26	11	4	3	30	14
1953-54	36	12	1	—	37	12
1954-55	22	7	3	1	25	8
	380	182	42	26	422	208

ENGLAND: 1948 v Switzerland; 1949 v Sweden, France, Northern Ireland, Italy; 1952 v Scotland (6 caps).

CHAPTER FIVE

Duncan Edwards

Duncan Edwards died in a Munich hospital at the tender age of 21, but already he had revealed enough to be regarded as possibly the greatest of the greats.

Certainly there are no doubts about his standing in the game in the mind of Jimmy Murphy, the Manchester United assistant manager who signed him as a sleepy-eyed schoolboy in pyjamas in the middle of the night and then watched him take the football world by storm until his tragically early death from his injuries in the Munich air crash.

As Jimmy so poignantly recalls in his own book: 'If I shut my eyes I can see him now. Those pants hitched up, the wild leaps of boyish enthusiasm as he came running out of the tunnel, the tremendous power of his tackle — always fair but fearsome — the immense power on the ball.

'In fact the number of times he was robbed of the ball once he had it at his feet could be counted on one hand. He was that sort of player. A players' player. Ask Bobby Charlton and he will tell you: "The greatest? There was only one, Duncan Edwards."

'When I hear Mohammed Ali proclaim on television and radio: "I am the greatest" I have to smile. You see, the greatest of them all was an English footballer named Duncan Edwards. The real professional.

'Any manager lucky enough to have him had half a team. And that is why, when I heard the sad news of Duncan's death on the morning of Friday, February 21, 1958, I broke down and cried. The club and England had lost a great footballer. I had lost a friend, a very dear friend.'

Duncan Edwards . . . the greatest of the great.

Duncan Edwards was indeed a giant, not just of stature, though this of course was a tremendous asset, but with an extraordinary ability for a big man. He was the complete all-rounder and on the basis that a good big 'un will always beat a good little 'un, he had a lot going for him.

He certainly stood out as a youngster. As Murphy puts it: 'From the first time I saw him as a boy of 14, he looked liked and played with the assurance of a man, with legs like tree trunks, a deep and powerful chest and an unforgettable zest for the game.

'He played wing half, centre half, centre forward and inside forward with the consummate ease of a great player.

He was never bothered where he played. He was quite simply a soccer Colossus.'

His achievements by the age of 21 speak for themselves. He was the youngest ever professional to play in the First Division when he was given his League debut against Cardiff City at Old Trafford on April 4, 1953, at the age of 16 years and 185 days.

The game was in fact lost 4-1 and he didn't play again that season, but it was a start and there was to be no holding him the following season when Matt Busby unveiled his Busby Babes in their full glory.

He went on to win championship medals in 1956 and 1957, and he played in the final of the F.A. Cup in 1957. He had also tasted European football with telling effect.

On the international front he was the youngest to play for England when he was given his first cap in April, 1955, to play against Scotland at Wembley aged 18 years and eight months.

This debut was certainly auspicious as England romped to a 7-2 victory, their biggest against the Scots in a peace-time fixture.

By the time of his death he had already won 18 caps, and after captaining the England schoolboys and Under-23 team, he was the obvious choice to follow Billy Wright as captain of his country.

Indeed the magnitude of what he might have achieved beggars description, because in addition to being blessed with exceptional physique and talent, he had the temperament and character to sustain a career.

Everyone who knew him speaks of his unassuming nature, his modesty, even his shyness, and the nice way he handled his early acclaim.

Manchester United learned right from the start that despite being wooed by nearly every top club in the country, his feet remained very much on the ground. In fact he proved to be one of their easiest signings.

Although as a schoolboy he had indicated that he wanted to come to Old Trafford, there was a last-minute

Duncan aged 16 but already with the physique of a man.

scare with a call from United's scout in the Midlands saying that another club were stepping up their efforts to get his signature.

Born at Dudley, his local big club, Wolves, had also long been after him and United had always feared that Stan Cullis would take him to Molineux.

The result was that when the emergency call came from the scout, United coach Bert Whalley drove through the night to the Edwards home and knocked the family up in the early hours.

Duncan came downstairs in his pyjamas to say: 'What's all the fuss about? I've already said Manchester United are the only club I want to join.'

And so he signed on the dotted line, as he said he would, though it still left a lot of people, especially at Wolves, wondering how United had done the trick at the expense of the Molineux club who of course were just as successful as Manchester United around that time.

Not to put too fine a point on it, the suspicion was that United had paid money to get him to Manchester, but Busby says the explanation is much simpler . . . the boy simply wanted to play for Manchester.

Sir Matt tells the story: 'I remember one particularly great display by Duncan on the Wolves' ground, and the inquest in the boardroom when it was all over. Stan Cullis said: "Matt, I'd like to know how you managed to sign Edwards. We thought he was all lined up to join Wolves."

'I told Stan: "I got Duncan in the same way you got Colin Booth. Young Colin is a Manchester boy, and I was with his parents the night before he joined Wolverhampton Wanderers. He was supposed to be joining Manchester United — but I don't hold that against you, Stan." The boy just wanted to go to Wolves.'

Once at Old Trafford, Edwards soon impressed and made an immediate impact among his contemporaries. He was a natural for the F.A. Youth Cup, a competition launched for season 1952-53, his first at the club.

He played a big part helping United establish themselves as the masters of the F.A. Youth Cup. United won the competition for five successive seasons from its inception, and Edwards played in the first three.

The first year United beat Wolves of all people in the final 9-3 over two legs. No wonder Stan Cullis was cross about losing him! The second season also saw Wolves in the final with Edwards rubbing more salt into the wound by scoring twice in a 5-4 aggregate win.

By the time of the third year Edwards was well established in the first team, but he liked nothing better than to turn out for his contemporaries and he played in the final to help notch a crushing 7-1 victory over West Bromwich in the two legs.

The up-and-coming Busby Babes toast their first success, the League championship of season 1955-56. Left to right: Duncan Edwards, Ian Greaves, Ray Wood, Dennis Viollet, Mark Jones, David Pegg and Eddie Colman.

He was almost unstoppable at this level. In one tie at Chelsea Jimmy Murphy had given the boys their pre-match instructions, urging them to remember that it was a team game and that they should play their normal game without being too conscious that Edwards was in the side.

At half-time they were a goal down, so he told them to forget what he had said and that they should look for Duncan and give him the ball. They did and he scored twice for a 2-1 victory.

Murphy also loves to recall a match at Charlton and the stick he was taking from the home fans on the apparently quiet performance from his star player.

'We ain't seen 'im, mate,' shouted one Cockney. But even as he spoke Edwards hit one from 40 yards and as it bulleted into the back of the Charlton net, Murphy was able to turn round and declare: 'There, my friend, is Duncan Edwards!'

Of course Duncan arrived at Old Trafford at the start of the golden age as the Busby Babes were prepared for that dramatic moment in October, 1953, when Matt Busby decided to give youth a fling.

He brought Edwards, Dennis Viollet and Jackie Blanchflower into the team against Huddersfield at the expense of some of the old guard, Stan Pearson, Henry Cockburn and Harry McShane.

Jeff Whitefoot and Bill Foulkes had already been introduced and David Pegg was soon to follow. The following season saw Billy Whelan and Mark Jones complete the takeover to lay the basis for the championship success of 1955-56.

Tommy Taylor, the one major buy surrounded by Busby's homespun team, led the charge up front to score 25 goals with 20 from Viollet and nine from Pegg.

Edwards, after flirting with an inside forward role, had settled into his best position at left half and was like a powerhouse unleashed.

The championship team mostly lined up: Wood, Foulkes, Byrne, Whitefoot/Colman, Jones, Edwards, Berry, Docherty/Whelan, Taylor, Viollet, Pegg.

Jackie Blanchflower, Colin Webster and Ian Greaves also figured for spells.

The team which took the title 11 points ahead of second-placed Blackpool had an average age of barely 22 . . . Busby Babes indeed with Duncan Edwards typifying the spirit and style of a side ready to tackle anything.

They built on their success by winning the championship the following season as well, this time romping home eight points in front of Spurs.

The team had settled down to read: Wood, Foulkes, Byrne, Colman, Jones, Edwards, Berry, Whelan, Taylor, Viollet, Pegg.

Their scoring topped the ton with the help of 26 from Billy Whelan, 22 from Tommy Taylor and 16 from Dennis Viollet.

Jackie Blanchflower came in for a few games, but the

Manchester United broke new ground for English football when they competed in the European Cup. Here they are poolside on the Continent. Left to right: Colin Webster, Eddie Colman, Wilf McGuinness, Jackie Blanchflower, Mark Jones, Ray Wood, Bobby Charlton, Duncan Edwards. In front with camera at the ready is Billy Whelan.

season was also notable for the introduction of yet another Babe, Bobby Charlton, who helped himself to 10 goals from 14 appearances.

Duncan Edwards made 34 appearances and scored five goals, providing the perfect balance with his power in contrast to the more delicate skills of Eddie 'Snakehips' Colman on the other flank.

The versatile nature of his football was revealed in the F.A. Cup as the Reds roared along to Wembley looking a sure-fire bet to achieve a League and Cup double.

The title was already in the bag when they walked out at Wembley to do battle with Aston Villa after some convincing wins with Edwards a particular hero in the fifth round when he had scored for a 1-0 win against Everton at Old Trafford.

United were firm favourites to win at Wembley.

'I have never been so sure of anything when I walked down the stairs of our hotel on the morning of the final,' says Sir Matt as he looks back on one of his major disappointments.

What the manager didn't know of course was that Peter McParland would crash into Ray Wood, leaving the goalkeeper with a broken cheekbone which forced him out of the match after only six minutes.

Jackie Blanchflower took over in goal and Duncan Edwards switched to centre half. The team performed valiantly and Tommy Taylor headed a fine goal but Wembley is no place for 10 men, even with a good team, and McParland broke through twice to score on each occasion.

Towards the end Busby sent a dazed Wood back on to the pitch and the players responded by recapturing some of their normal rhythm, but they lost 2-1.

United were obviously bitterly disappointed, but there was no denying the greatness of their team, as they also showed in the European arena.

Matt Busby had defied the authority of the F.A. and League to take his club into the European Cup as champions, partly because he saw football as a global game, but also, I suspect, because he knew he had a team capable of succeeding where England on the international stage had been failing.

He was right, too, with his young gladiators reaching the semi-finals in their first Continental campaign, and only falling against the experience and silky Spanish skills of Real Madrid.

Always relishing these European battles and always in the thick of it was Edwards. Even when United lost the first leg of their semi-final 3-1 in Madrid, 'Old International' in *The Guardian* referred to the 'oak-tree strength of Edwards'.

His shots packed so much power that the Germans once nicknamed him 'Boom Boom'. He had impressed them so

Two young men perhaps drinking a toast to friendship and success for Manchester United. Tragically Duncan Edwards (left) and Tommy Taylor both lost their lives soon after in the Munich air crash.

much playing in an English 3-1 victory in Germany that when United landed in West Berlin a few months later for a pre-season tour, the German fans were all calling for Boom Boom.

International football always used to pose a dilemma for Jimmy Murphy, especially when England were playing Wales. Before one particular match Jimmy, as the Welsh manager, was detailing the strengths and weaknesses of the England team, running through the opposition one by one.

He mentioned them all except Edwards, which left Reg Davies, the Newcastle inside forward, feeling a little out of it because he was in direct opposition to the United wing half.

'What about Edwards?' questioned Davies.

Replied Murphy: 'Just keep out of his way, son, there's nothing I could say which would help us.'

Bobby Charlton remembers Duncan with particular affection, not just as a footballer and friend, but as a soldier. They both spent part of their National Service at the same unit.

Bobby recalls in his book *My Soccer Life:* 'I remember playing with him once in an Army Cup tie. We were 4-2 down with the game nearly over. So Duncan switched to centre forward. In 10 minutes he scored four and we won 7-4.

'I quote that example of him in a relatively unimportant match because I think it supplies the key to his genius. For Duncan, you see, there was no such thing as an unimportant match. In one season he played nearly a hundred games for United, England and the Army — and he gave 100 per cent in the lot.

'I don't say he intended to. There were probably small-time Army games when he thought he would have a quiet cruise through — just keep out of trouble and not over-tire himself for the next international or League match.

'But once the game started everything else went out of his mind. He ran and tackled and surged through as if his reputation depended upon it.

'Whether it was at Wembley or on a bumpy pitch behind the barracks, he became immersed in it.'

Bobby remembers joining United as a youngster and when he met Jimmy Murphy for the first time found his boss talking non-stop about the attributes of a fellow called Edwards.

'I wondered why he was bothering with me if this Edwards was so good. Later I understood why Jimmy couldn't stop talking about him.

'He was the greatest. I see him in my mind's eye and wonder that anyone should have so much talent. He had the sort of build a boxer pines for. He was a shade under six feet, and weighed about 13 and a half stone. He was a hard tough man in the tackle, but he was also a shrewd intelligent player.

The stained-glass window in memory of Duncan Edwards in St Francis's Church, Dudley, where he was born.

'His other exceptional quality was that he always liked to be winning or saving matches. He had a shot that could burst through the best goalkeeper's hands yet, when the pressure was on his own goalmouth, he would be back there battling away.

'He had that sort of speed which made that possible and ensured that he was never caught out of position. One minute he would be clearing off his line, the next surging through at the other end.

'He was out on his own at left half, and a First Division player in every other position.'

Duncan's last match on British soil was in the spectacular 5-4 League victory at Arsenal shortly before flying out to Belgrade for the second leg of their European Cup quarter-final against Red Star.

Duncan scored a typical goal at Highbury to give United the lead. By half-time they led 3-0. In the second half Arsenal fought back to make it 3-3 and set the scene for a dramatic finish which saw United step up a gear again to win 5-4.

It was audacious, thrilling football which reflected the attitude of the Busby Babes who featured yet two more talented youngsters with Albert Scanlon and Kenny Morgans playing on the wings.

If a footballing epitaph was needed to express the power and the glory of the 21-year-old Duncan Edwards and his team-mates, then it was unforgettably etched at Highbury that day.

The team lined up: Gregg, Foulkes, Byrne, Colman, Jones, Edwards, Morgans, Charlton, Taylor, Viollet, Charlton.

A few hours later and the United party flew out to Yugoslavia protecting a 2-1 lead from the first leg at Old Trafford, and after sailing into a 3-0 lead with two goals from Bobby Charlton and one from Dennis Viollet the tie looked to be in the bag.

Once again, though, United flirted with the result and let Red Star in to score three goals for a 3-3 draw on the night. But they were through on aggregate, and it was a happy party which prepared for the fateful flight back home.

The weather was so bad that Edwards, always thoughtful and caring, sent a telegram to his landlady in Gorse Avenue, Stretford, saying 'All flights cancelled flying tomorrow — Duncan.'

Tragically they did fly and crashed on the runway at Munich attempting to take off after a refuelling stop. Seven of the players were killed along with three members of staff. Eight of the nine sports writers on board lost their lives. One of the crew and two other passengers also perished.

The co-pilot died later in hospital and so, too, did Duncan Edwards after bravely fighting for his life for 15 days.

Frank Taylor, the surviving journalist who like Matt Busby had also been grievously injured, said later that it was only Duncan's 'stupendous spirit' that had kept him battling for as long as he did.

One of the surgeons at the Rechts der Isar Hospital said: 'I have seen death many, many times, but not like this. In all my years I have never seen a hospital staff so upset. This boy we have never seen before, he comes to our hospital — but he is so young, so strong . . . so brave. Ach, but he had no chance.'

Walter Winterbottom, the England manager, said in tribute: 'Duncan was a great footballer and he had the promise of becoming the greatest of his day. He played with tremendous joy and his spirit stimulated the whole England team. It was in the character and spirit of Duncan Edwards that I saw the true revival of British football.'

As Frank Taylor wrote in his book: 'There were many tears that day in Munich, and far beyond, for a boy who had taken the world of sport by storm; who epitomized the power and zest and all that's best in British sport. A worthy young sports idol for the youth of the nation. Duncan Edwards was unforgettable.

'So long, Dunc. It was great while it lasted.'

DUNCAN EDWARDS' RECORD

	LEAGUE		F.A. CUP		EUROPE		TOTAL	
	App	Gls	App	Gls	App	Gls	App	Gls
1952-53	1						1	
1953-54	24		1				25	
1954-55	33	6	3				36	6
1955-56	33	3					33	3
1956-57	34	5	6	1	7		47	6
1957-58	26	6	2		5		33	6
	151	20	12	1	12		175	21

ENGLAND: 1955 v Sotland, France, Spain, Portugal; 1956 v Scotland, Brazil, Sweden, Finland, West Germany, Northern Ireland, Denmark; 1957 v Scotland, Republic of Ireland, Denmark, Republic of Ireland, Wales, Northern Ireland, France (18 caps).

CHAPTER SIX

Bobby Charlton

Bobby Charlton in full stride unleashing one of his thunderous shots conjures up possibly my favourite image of football, as I imagine it does for thousands of people who love the game.

There was no more majestic sight than Charlton, his cheeks puffed with the effort, bearing down on goal. There was a grace and beauty about his game which captured the true sporting spirit.

The added bonus was that we watched an idol without feet of clay, a hero who represented all the good things of professional soccer. He played the game, and he played it well.

As Geoffrey Green timelessly put it in his book, *There's Only One United:* 'His flowing movements when surging into attack suggested a hidden poetic line: the ceaseless support for each colleague on the field, while himself was rotating as the midfield hub of the wheel, reflected a selfless loyalty to a cause; his high standard of behaviour on stage still remains an example and a reproach to others in a game of violence, and as such remains a mirror of deeper values.

'In a long career, he carved a name as a chivalrous scrupulous opponent. Yet it was the explosive facets of his play that will remain fresh in memory. His thinning fair hair streaming in the wind, he moved like a ship in full sail. He always possessed an elemental quality, jinking, changing feet and direction, turning gracefully on the ball, or accelerating through a gap surrendered by a confused enemy, he could be gone like the wind.'

Now after a distinguished playing career for Manchester

United and England he has moved just as successfully into a new phase of his life which sees him as a teacher, a fitting role for a man who regards Old Trafford as a theatre of dreams.

He is a partner in a travel business with the accent on sport, but I imagine his real joy is in his work as principal of the Bobby Charlton Sports Schools.

Started originally as purely a soccer school for boys, his courses now embrace all the sports and attract youngsters from as far away as China.

A thoughtful and fluent speaker, he's a splendid ambassador for football, and his qualities have not been lost on Manchester United who invited him to become a director in recognition not just of his past service but for the contribution he can make to the future of the club.

Bobby has come a long way since his early days at Ashington Junior School where his first football shorts were run up by one of the lady teachers from wartime blackout curtaining.

Not that football wasn't in his blood. Born in Northumberland the son of a miner in the coal pit village of Ashington, his mother, Cissie, came from the well-known Milburn soccer family.

Three uncles, Jack, Jim and George, played for Leeds United. Uncle Stan played for Leicester City and his mother's cousin, the great Jackie Milburn, was Newcastle United's legendary centre forward of the 1950s. Grandfather 'Tanner' Milburn was a goalkeeper.

Hardly surprisingly, the two Charlton brothers, Bobby and Jack, were soon progressing through their school teams. Jack was to find fame with Leeds and England, but it was Bobby who attracted the early attention.

Happily for Manchester United, they were one of the first clubs to go knocking on his door after their chief scout, little Joe Armstrong, had come hurrying back to Manchester one day to report: 'I had to peer through a mist, but what I saw was enough. This boy is going to be a world beater.'

Bobby Charlton, now a director of Manchester United after a distinguished playing career.

Later when he had begun to bang in goals for the England schoolboy team, scouts from many clubs came calling, but Bobby remembered the man who had shown the first interest and he chose to join United.

He first caught the public's eye in Manchester as part of the young explosion which saw United win the F.A. Youth Cup five years in succession from its inception in season 1952-53. Bobby played in three of those successful campaigns.

He was always outstanding as a youngster, but the coaching staff reveal now that the diamond took a lot of polishing before his talents could be harnessed for professional football.

Jimmy Murphy recalls: 'Bobby was a difficult pupil. He did so many things superbly and by instinct, but he kept spoiling it by hitting long balls to right or left wing and then standing still. It was beautiful to watch, and yet so many of the long passes were made when a short one would have been better.

'Bert Whalley and I used to tell him: "Before you become a good long ball player, son, you must first master the short game." To his eternal credit Bobby never shirked these training sessions.'

Bobby Charlton also remembers going through the Murphy mangle squeezing him into shape. 'Jimmy used to play in practice matches with us and he used to come up behind me and kick me on the back of my legs. I used to wonder what on earth was going on. Now when I look back I realise he was trying to toughen me up to take the knocks — and to encourage me to pass the ball a bit quicker,' he said.

He certainly proved an apt pupil, though he had to wait what he considered to be an inordinate length of time for his League debut.

Bobby told me: 'I thought I was never going to get into the first team. I was scoring a lot of goals in the reserves and I kept thinking surely Matt Busby would play me soon.

'Everyone kept telling me I would play, but it never seemed to happen until just before a home match against Charlton Athletic when the Boss asked me if I was OK.

'Actually I wasn't because I had sprained my ankle playing for the reserves, but I wasn't going to admit it. I said I was fine and crossed my fingers. So Mr Busby said I would be playing the next day.

'I carried the leg a little, but it went well for me and I managed to score twice, one goal from close in and the other from outside the box. We won 4-2, but I was still dropped for the following game.

'I had only played because Tommy Taylor had been injured. He was fit again so I had to go out. It just showed how severe the competition for places was around that time.

Manchester United proudly parade their dream trophy, the European Cup. 'Defeat was never in our minds,' says Bobby Charlton.
Back row: Bill Foulkes, Johnny Aston, Jimmy Rimmer, Alex Stepney, Alan Gowling, David Herd.
Middle: David Sadler, Tony Dunne, Shay Brennan, Pat Crerand, George Best, Francis Burns, Jack Crompton (trainer).
Front: Jimmy Ryan, Nobby Stiles, Denis Law, Matt Busby (manager), Bobby Charlton, Brian Kidd, John Fitzpatrick.

'Actually I got back into the team the next game because this time Dennis Viollet was injured, and that's how it went for the rest of the season, in and out whenever there was injury to one of our forwards like Tommy Taylor, Dennis Viollet or Billy Whelan.'

Bobby's League debut was on October 6, 1956, and he made a total of 14 League appearances and scored 10 goals to make a valuable contribution to the Busby Babes' first championship success.

He also played in the later stages of the F.A. Cup that season, scoring in the semi-final win against Birmingham City and then playing at Wembley in the ill-fated final against Aston Villa when Ray Wood had his cheekbone smashed and United lost 2-1.

The 18-year-old Charlton also made his entry in the European Cup, playing in the second-leg 2-2 draw against Real Madrid in the semi-final. It was a vintage season, of course, as the Busby Babes made the football world sit up and take notice.

The team had scored 103 goals to win the championship, and Bobby's 10 paled alongside the 26 scored by Billy Whelan, the 22 by Tommy Taylor and Dennis Viollet's 16.

Nevertheless it was a sparkling start, though he still faced a fight for a regular place in the first team which didn't come until a couple of months before the Munich accident in the February of the following season.

Then there was no looking back, and in the seven games he played between mid-December and the air crash he scored seven goals, including a hat-trick in a 7-2 win over Bolton Wanderers at Old Trafford. He also scored both goals in an F.A. Cup fourth-round 2-0 success against Ipswich.

He was on the scoresheet in Europe at this stage as well. He got one of the goals in the first leg of their European Cup quarter-final against Red Star when they established a 2-1 advantage.

He scored twice in the 3-3 draw in Belgrade as the Busby Babes sailed along in three competitions with the football world seemingly at their feet.

Then everything came to an abrupt full stop . . . the Busby Babes destroyed at Munich on February 6, 1958, the greatest English club side, says Bobby, he had ever seen.

The Elizabethan two-engined plane crashed on its third attempt to take off from the slushy runway at the snow-covered airfield. It was nearly three o'clock in the afternoon and everyone was tense and quiet.

In his book *My Soccer Life* Bobby writes: 'We went down the runway again with the fields slipping past the window as we gathered speed. I thought: "We're taking a long time getting off." Then I saw a fence at the end of the runway

Bobby Charlton after being presented with his European Footballer of the Year trophy at Old Trafford.

and I knew we couldn't clear it. I didn't know what was beyond it. I just saw the fence rushing at us and then the bang as we knocked it over.

'After that there was nothing. No noise, no heroics . . . best of all no memories.

'I came to yards away from the plane. I was still strapped in my seat. Everywhere there was slush and water . . . desolation and misery. I thought I had only blacked out for seconds, but I must have been unconscious for 10 minutes or more. Harry Gregg had already been back into the plane to help the injured.

'I saw the house then. We must have hit it. People in fire

helmets were running towards us and screaming. Flames were flickering round the front of the plane. Dennis Viollet was next to me. He too was still in his seat. Some of the lads were lying around. Nobody was moving. I didn't think anything because there was nothing to think. Everything was still and stricken so that it was like being in the middle of a painting.

'The Boss was lying a little way from us. He started to sit up but he was having trouble with his legs. I released the seat belt and walked over to see him. Jackie Blanchflower was next to him. I felt unhurt.

'Four of us had been thrown out into the slush. I can only guess that the plane had spun round as the wing touched the house and tipped us out. Somebody put me and Dennis into a car and rushed us to the airport centre. From the airport we went to hospital.'

Bobby was cut about the head and hands as well as suffering from concussion and shock. He learned who had died and who had survived from a German in the next bed reading from a newspaper, but nothing seemed very clear to him.

After a fortnight in hospital he arrived back in England where he was sent home to Ashington by Jimmy Murphy. For while Bill Foulkes and Harry Gregg carried on in football straight away, the 20-year-old Charlton was still somewhat in a daze.

He came back to Manchester in time to watch the first game after Munich when the patched-up team played Sheffield Wednesday in the fifth round of the F.A. Cup just 13 days after the crash.

They had had to leave blanks in the programme on the team line-up page because no-one knew until the last minute who would be playing. It was an emotion-charged night as United swept to a 3-0 victory in front of a packed Old Trafford.

'Had we lost,' says Bobby, 'I think Manchester would have died of a broken heart.'

At the same time Bobby realised he was ready to play

Celebration time at Wembley as England win the World Cup in 1966. Back row: Jack Charlton, Gordon Banks, Roger Hunt, Bobby Moore, Geoff Hurst, George Cohen, Bobby Charlton. Front: Alan Ball, Martin Peters, Ray Wilson.

again and the following Monday he was back at the ground in light training. He wasn't picked for the following League game, but Jimmy Murphy brought him in to play at outside left in the next round of the F.A. Cup against West Bromwich.

The game at The Hawthorns was drawn 2-2, but Bobby was playing again and he helped knock the Albion out at Old Trafford in the replay with a long run and a pass to Colin Webster for the Welshman to score the goal in a 1-0 win.

From then on it was a helter-skelter of emotions as the patched-up team completed the rest of the League season to finish in ninth place and reach the final of the F.A. Cup on a tide of emotion.

The fairy tale ended at Wembley with a 2-0 win for Bolton Wanderers. Nat Lofthouse got both goals, the second as a result of charging Harry Gregg and the ball over the line in what was probably a foul, but Bolton were really the better team while United looked drained, and understandably so.

United's Cup-final team lined up:
Gregg, Foulkes, Greaves, Goodwin, Cope, Crowther, Dawson, Taylor, Charlton, Viollett, Scanlon.

Then began the long and difficult process of rebuilding, but with Bobby Charlton, who had gone into Munich a boy and emerged a man, prepared to bear a heavier responsibility.

In the season after Munich he played 38 League games and scored 29 goals from inside left. The team finished runners-up to Wolves for the championship, an incredible performance considering the ravages of Munich. Not surprisingly they dipped for a season or two after that. Players came and went; Charlton was a constant, though, first in his pre-Munich role of inside forward, then as an outside left, a position he didn't enjoy because he wasn't involved enough in the game.

He was on the wing in the team which beat Leicester to win the F.A. Cup in 1963, but he was back at inside forward to help win the championship in 1964-65.

It was a star-studded attack with John Connelly and George Best on the wings, David Herd and Denis Law the strikers and Bobby knitting the whole thing together in midfield alongside Pat Crerand.

The team were slowly building to a peak and they won the League again in 1966-67, with Bobby Charlton an ever-present, to set themselves up for their triumph in the European Cup of 1968.

Bobby felt it was United's destiny to become champions of Europe that season, exactly 10 years after Munich.

He recalls: 'My thoughts on the day of the final against Benfica were that we just couldn't lose. I can remember thinking that we had come too far and been through too much for us to fail in that final game.

'We had everything going for us. We were on our own patch at Wembley. We had a good record against teams from Portugal, and after coming from 3-1 down in Madrid

In 17 seasons of first-team football Bobby Charlton made a club record 604 League appearances and became a sporting idol who represented all the good things of professional soccer.

to get through the semi-final I thought it would be impossible for us to get beaten.

'It was very humid on the day of the final and I knew it would be hard work, but I also knew that we would find something extra. That's a quality British teams have always had, a resilience, especially in extra time, just as England had shown to win the World Cup two years before.

'We should have been dead and buried in the semi-final against Real Madrid when we were 3-1 down, and the fact that we had come back and beaten them gave us all an invincible feeling.

'I thought there was no point me worrying because Benfica had a lot more to worry about.

'I had been very disappointed in some of our other semi-final performances, especially the one against Partizan. We had a good team in 1966, and losing 2-0 over there had been bad news.

'I knew it would come one day, yet it was in the nick of time. Without being disrespectful to the players involved, the 1968 team was not our best.

'Manchester City had won the League and we had faded. A lot of us were past our peak. I knew I wasn't going to get another chance and about half the team were in the same boat.

'But as I say, defeat was never in our minds. Our first goal confirmed the thought because I scored it with a header — and that never happened very often.

'We felt some despair when they equalised to force us into extra time. But even then I thought that our background of stamina training would stand us in good stead. We knew they must be tired as well.

'Then came that sparkling 10 minutes in which we scored three goals . . . George Best, Brian Kidd and I turned in the final one.

'Benfica were a formidable side going forward but I thought their defence might creak, and that's how it worked out. Our defence rose to the occasion with some key saves from Alex Stepney against Eusebio, and steady displays from Bill Foulkes, Shay Brennan and Tony Dunne.

'Nobby Stiles was an important cog in that team. He used to tidy up for us. He seemed able to sense trouble and

Just before the kick-off against Northern Ireland in April, 1970, Bobby was presented with a special plaque to mark his 100th game for England.

where danger was going to come from. So he was always there, a great reader of the game.

'He was a bit like a sheepdog keeping everything under control. If one of the sheep tried to break away he would dart into action and put them back in the pen.

'Johnny Aston had a particularly good game in the final, running the legs off their full back to produce some great crosses. He pulled their defence wide which gave the rest of us more room.

'When the final whistle had gone I remember thinking that it was the ultimate achievement, not just for the individual players but for the club and Matt Busby.

'I suppose I can't speak for everyone, but at the same time I think I probably do, when I say that we felt that it had been a duty to the club.

'For some of us it had become a family thing. We had

been together so long, and while people recognised that we had had some great teams, there was nothing in the European record book until 1968 to show for it.

'Sir Matt had made us pioneers in Europe, and winning the European Cup was not just a Manchester occasion, it was for the whole country.

'I missed most of the celebrating that night. I was absolutely drained and kept fainting. I couldn't make the reception. Norma, my wife, told me that Matt had gone up late in the evening to sing "What a wonderful world", and I guess that just about summed it up for all of us.'

In all, Bobby Charlton had 17 seasons of First Division football for Manchester United to total a club record 604 League appearances and score a record 199 goals. Bill Foulkes had been the previous record holder with 563 League games to his name.

On the international front he held the England appearance record with 106 caps until Bobby Moore went two better, but he still holds the England scoring record with 49 goals. Jimmy Greaves had held the old record with 44 goals, and it is difficult to see anyone in the modern game — not even Gary Lineker — matching the Charlton figures.

He won his first cap a few months after Munich and altogether his international career spanned 12 years. The highspot was of course in 1966 when he helped England to win the World Cup. He scored two great goals against Portugal to put his country into the final against Germany at Wembley when he gave a masterly display to share in the 4-2 extra-time victory.

The same year he was voted England's Footballer of the Year by the soccer writers, an honour quickly followed by European Footballer of the Year, finishing ahead of such luminaries as Eusebio and Franz Beckenbauer.

He holds the OBE and is a CBE after an impeccably disciplined career in which his only booking was somehow lost, and understandably so.

His last game for Manchester United was a relatively

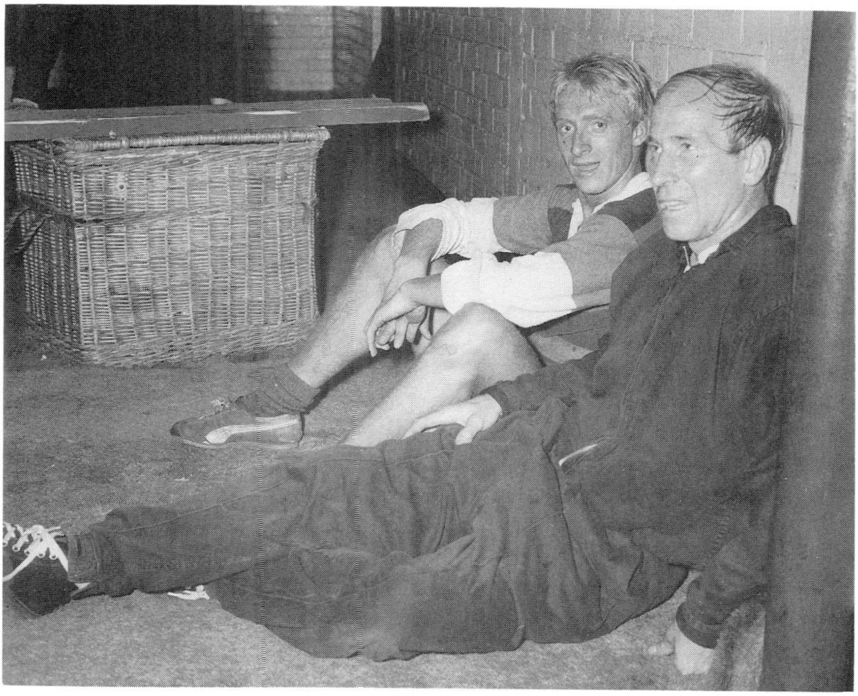

Football isn't just about glamour . . . there is the hard work and sweat of training as Bobby reveals here recovering from a particularly gruelling stint with Denis Law.

obscure fixture against Verona in Italy in the Anglo-Italian tournament at the end of the 1972-73 season. Nevertheless he scored twice in a 4-1 win.

He is still playing, appearing in testimonial matches and for the United old players association team . . . and moaning at his team-mates, I'm told, because he still doesn't like losing.

As Sir Matt Busby puts it: 'The name of Bobby Charlton will stand for ever. Time will undoubtedly add to his stature, rather than diminish it.

'He arrived at Old Trafford a shy, perhaps slightly bewildered boy of 15. The shy boy has blossomed now into a man with a great sense of assurance, confidence and responsibility.

'In the old days it seemed players were always wanting

transfers if things didn't go their way. They were often difficult to satisfy. I cannot remember Bobby Charlton ever having a moment's dissatisfaction.

'The only instance that comes to mind was the occasion when I offered him a two-year contract which was our normal period of service at that time. He inquired rather tentatively if I minded him having one for three years. My answer was that he could have a four-year contract.

'I had no hesitation because his heart and mind have been forever at Old Trafford, wrapped up in the interests of Manchester United.

'We trod the same road for a great part of our careers, aiming for the same achievements and sharing the disappointments as well as the triumphs. And when things looked their blackest after the Munich accident and there were times when I felt a great despair, I was cheered enormously to think that Bobby Charlton was there.

'He was one of the foundation stones and his presence was a great source of inspiration to keep working for the restoration of Manchester United.

'One of the delightful aspects of his character is that he has retained a tremendous enthusiasm. Losing always meant something to him as well as winning. It made him a better professional.

'His shyness never showed on the field of play. I remember the goals he scored when he was only 18. I have vividly implanted in my mind the sight of him volleying David Pegg's centre home in the F.A. Cup semi-final against Birmingham at Hillsborough. It was a tremendously hit shot and he repeated it in his first international playing for England against Scotland at Hampden.

'I can't begin to describe all the other wonderful goals he has scored or list his proud international career, except to say what a marvellous contribution he made in the World Cup of 1966 with his so valuable goals.

'Could I also ever forget his header in the final of the European Cup in 1968, a goal which set us on the path towards the victory that had been our aim for so long.

Farewell to football in 1973 as Bobby Charlton is applauded on to the pitch by Manchester United and Sheffield United players for a presentation to record his final League appearance at Old Trafford.

'He has broken all records and won everything possible there is to win. Yet he has remained completely unspoiled, still prepared to do more than his fair share for the cause of Manchester United.'

BOBBY CHARLTON'S RECORD

	LEAGUE		F.A. CUP		F.L. CUP		EUROPE		TOTAL	
	App	Gls	App	Gls	App	Gls	App	Gls	App	Gls
1956-57	14	10	2	1			1	1	17	12
1957-58	21	8	7	5			2	3	30	16
1958-59	38	29	1						39	29
1959-60	37	18	3	3					40	21
1960-61	39	21	3						42	21
1961-62	37	8	7	2					44	10
1962-63	28	7	6	2					34	9
1963-64	40	9	7	2			6	4	53	15
1964-65	41	10	7				11	8	59	18
1965-66	38	16	7				8	2	53	18
1966-67	42	12	2						44	12
1967-68	41	15	2	1			9	2	52	18
1968-69	32	5	6				8	2	46	7
1969-70	40	12	9	1	8	1			57	14
1970-71	42	5	2		6	3			50	8
1971-72	40	8	7	2	6	2			53	12
1972-73	34/2	6	1		4	1			39/2	7
	604/2	199	79	19	24	7	45	22	752/2	247

ENGLAND: 1958 v Scotland, Portugal, Yugoslavia, Northern Ireland, USSR, Wales; 1959 v Scotland, Italy, Brazil, Peru, Mexico, USA, Wales, Sweden; 1960 v Scotland, Yugoslavia, Spain, Hungary, Northern Ireland, Luxembourg, Spain, Wales; 1961 v Scotland, Mexico, Portugal, Italy, Austria, Luxembourg, Wales, Portugal, Northern Ireland; 1962 v Austria, Scotland, Switzerland, Peru, Hungary, Argentina, Bulgaria, Brazil; 1963 v France, Scotland, Brazil, Czechoslovakia, East Germany, Switzerland, Wales, Rest of World, Northern Ireland; 1964 v Scotland, Uruguay, Portugal, Republic of Ireland, USA (sub), Brazil, Argentina, Northern Ireland, Holland; 1965 v Scotland, Wales, Austria, Northern Ireland, Spain; 1966 v West Germany, Scotland, Yugoslavia, Finland, Norway, Poland, Uruguay, Mexico, France, Argentina, Portugal, West Germany, Northern Ireland, Czechoslovakia, Wales; 1967 v Scotland, Wales, Northern Ireland, USSR; 1968 v Scotland, Spain (twice), Sweden, Yugoslavia, USSR, Rumania, Bulgaria; 1969 v Rumania, Northern Ireland, Wales, Scotland, Mexico, Brazil, Holland, Portugal; 1970 v Holland, Wales, Northern Ireland, Colombia, Ecuador, Rumania, Brazil, Czechoslovakia, West Germany (106 caps).

CHAPTER SEVEN

Denis Law

Denis Law was the king and his subjects were the Stretford Enders.

No player has commanded more allegiance from the terrace fans than the man who proved the most deadly marksman of all the famous players to perform on the Old Trafford stage.

It wasn't just his prolific goal scoring that won their affection, it was his style and, I suspect, the streak of villainy which undoubtedly ran through his football.

The lads at the Stretford End found it easy to identify with a player whose commitment and aggression were so obvious. He was slightly built, but there was a venom in his play which brought him into confrontation with opponents and referees.

The crowd liked that; they love a man who brings not only skill to the game but a willingness to fly into the thick of the action with no holds barred.

Denis Law was daring, cocky, impudent and abrasive; he could play a bit as well and the whole explosive mixture made him the supreme people's champion.

The famous litany of Charlton, Law and Best still trips easily off the tongue. Each was a star in his own right. Charlton was admired and Best was fantastic, but Law was worshipped for the way he combined flair and fire.

Few who watched Manchester United in the Sixties will forget the Law trademark as he signalled his goals to the crowd, punching the air and then running with one arm raised, finger pointing to the sky. The crowd would rise to his salute as to a gladiator of old!

Goals are the name of the game of course and the

Lawman got them more often than anyone. His scoring rate was phenomenal.

Charlton was renowned for his cannonball shooting and he holds the club scoring record for his total of goals. Best was a wizard in front of goal and Dennis Viollet still holds the season's League record with 32 in 1959-60.

Jack Rowley, Stan Pearson, Tommy Taylor, David Herd, Joe Jordan, Stuart Pearson and Mark Hughes are just a few of the other outstanding marksmen to have worn a red shirt, but Law reigns supreme because of his incredible ratio of goals to appearances, especially in Cup football.

In the League Denis scored 171 goals in 305 games for United, well over the usual striker's target of a goal every two games.

Bobby Charlton scored 198 times, but it took him 604 games to do it; and for all his scoring magic George Best's tally was only in a ratio of 137 goals from 361 appearances.

I say 'only' but this is only in comparison with the best in the business and when you turn to Cup competition, Law had an astounding scoring rate.

In Europe he scored 28 goals in 33 matches and in the F.A. Cup he hit 34 goals from 44 ties. When Wembley beckoned he was lethal. He once scored six for Manchester City against Luton only to see them wiped off the record when the game was abandoned because of a waterlogged pitch.

But of course the figures only tell half the story and certainly don't explain why he was so lionised by the crowd. What the fans loved so much was the way he scored them with his spectacular overhead and scissors kicks, and his whiplash headers.

He jumped so high at times and seemed to hang there so long that it looked as if he had a sky-hook. He was lean and hungry with it, his courage never in question. Lightning over two or three yards, his reflexes were razor sharp.

Yet few would have predicted such a glittering career looking at Denis Law as a youngster.

Manchester United made Denis Law a happy man when they rescued him from Italian football and paid Torino a record £115,000.

Born in Aberdeen the youngest of seven children, life was fairly hard. His father spent his working life on the trawlers fishing out of the port and there were few luxuries. His pal gave him his first pair of football boots so that he could play for the school Under-11 team. He remembers vividly his first new pair, bought on credit by his Mum when he was 13.

'I caught the tram and went down to the city centre on a cloud. I bought myself a pair of Hotspur boots — I can see them now, they had big ankle protectors and were as hard as a brick. I can remember when I got home sitting on the sink with my feet in a basin of water to soften the leather. I could hardly believe my luck,' says Denis.

The boots were cleaned, dried, dubbined and cherished as young Denis graduated to play for Aberdeen Schoolboys, and was picked on one occasion as a reserve for the Scotland team.

At top level he had a lot against him. For Denis had

inherited a family affliction which caused him no end of misery as a youngster. From the age of five his right eye was badly crossed and he had to wear glasses to correct the squint.

When he played football, though, he couldn't wear glasses so he adopted the technique of going through an entire match with his right eye tightly closed. He was in fact a one-eyed footballer, an experience which might well have accounted for the competitive, abrasive streak which ran through his game.

Denis admits: 'With a handicap you had to be harder and stand up and fight, and the only way I could fight was to go out on the pitch and play football.'

He attracted the attention of Archie Beattie whose brother Andy was manager of Huddersfield Town and he was invited for a trial at the Leeds Road club.

'I couldn't really believe that Huddersfield Town were likely to be very impressed by me when they saw me. After all, I was only a skinny bit of a kid weighing little more than eight stone, and I still had my squint and my owl-like glasses, although by then I did have my name on a waiting list for an operation to correct the defect,' was the Law verdict.

But Huddersfield liked what they saw and took him on to their ground staff. After a few months he went back home to Aberdeen for his operation which was a complete success, though right through his career the vision in his right eye was always blurred.

The main thing, though, was that he could now play football without having to screw up one eye, and as Denis says: 'I could now open both eyes without having to look in two directions at once. It was like a miracle.

'I've been told that I had a bit of a swagger on the football field. Well, that was the day it started. That operation completely changed my life. I strutted out of the hospital with my chest stuck out, no hurdle in life would be too great to climb from now on.'

Bill Shankly, later Huddersfield's manager, but then in

For a slightly built player Denis Law was spectacular in the air and looked at times as if he had his own personal skyhook.

charge of the reserves, had not been too impressed by his first sighting of Law.

'He looked like a skinned rabbit. My first reaction was to say get him on the next train home.

'But from the first moment I saw him play I realised that here was something special. There was never any danger that he wasn't going to make it,' declared Shanks.

Shankly soon had him playing in the reserves and on

Christmas Eve, 1956, he was given his League debut at Notts County aged 16 years and 10 months.

Shankly arranged for the cafe opposite the Huddersfield ground to feed him up on a special diet of steaks and milk. He was still as thin as a rake, but what he lacked in chunky muscle he made up for with his lightning speed off the mark, his instant reactions and of course his aggression.

He oozed a natural arrogance which demanded a bigger stage.

Matt Busby tried to give him one after Manchester United's youth team had played Huddersfield in the F.A. Youth Cup. He offered £10,000 but it was turned down. Matt was obviously impressed and in October 1958, he gave Denis his first Scottish cap, making him the youngest since Bob McColl in 1899.

Huddersfield were only a Second Division club at the time so it was a bold decision. Denis went on to play for Scotland 55 times, scoring 30 goals, a good enough record, though the player feels he might have done better for his country.

'Injuries didn't help me very much in my international career. I played a few times when I wasn't fully fit. You can get away with it at club level but not in internationals. I'm very proud to have played for Scotland. There is nothing quite like pulling on a Scottish jersey, but I would like to have done more.'

Back at Huddersfield it was clear he was going to move on, and Manchester City were the club who dug deep to find £56,000 for a young player with only 81 League appearances to his name.

Denis only stayed at Maine Road for two seasons before the chance of a big profit proved too much for City who would have found it extremely difficult anyway to stand in the way of a dream move to Italy.

Denis had done his stuff for City with 21 League goals in 44 appearances, a scoring rate which brought Torino in with a £100,000 offer.

It had been hard work, too, and had brought any number of clashes over training methods.

Denis Law was 'The King' as far as the Stretford Enders were concerned and they loved his spectacular goals and scissors kicks.

'Apart from Bert Trautmann, only Ken Barnes and George Hannah could really play,' says Denis.

'I knew that if I stayed with City we faced the prospect of a continued fight against relegation. I wanted to go to Italy. There was a feeling that Italy was the place where it was all happening, that it was becoming the mecca of European football. John Charles had been with Juventus for four years, and now Gigi Peronace was back in England looking for more British talent.'

Denis admits that lira was the lure. The kind of money on offer was a £5,000 signing-on fee plus big bonuses like £200 for a win. It compared handsomely with the English maximum wage of £20, though this was about to be scrapped, and in fact City offered Denis £80 a week to stay.

But the financial dream became a nightmare; the money

didn't turn out to be quite as good as promised, and Italian football was a disaster. Although Torino had also signed Joe Baker from Hibs and they had each other for company, they were bored and lonely off the field, while on it they found the Italian football an alien game.

The fans and the Press made their lives unbearable and they were always in trouble and being fined by the club. Joe Baker so disliked being taken away into the mountains above Turin in preparation for matches that he went on a hunger strike, and much to the delight of the other players, the system was scrapped.

Their most horrendous experience was when Joe turned his new car over going the wrong way round a roundabout and suffered severe head injuries with Denis fortunate to escape being crushed.

The final nail in the coffin was when Denis was pulled off the pitch in a Cup tie and accused of not trying because of a Scotland international which was coming up. Torino refused him permission to play in it and it proved the last straw for the Italian adventure.

Explains the player: 'It wasn't long before I realised I had made a ghastly mistake. I'm not one for the high life, but it was like a prison. All I wanted really was to be treated like a human being. It all finally blew up when Torino refused to release me to play for Scotland.

'That was the end as far as I was concerned. I stormed out so quickly that I left all my clothes behind, and I never saw them again.'

Back in Scotland for the international, Denis contacted Matt Busby to tell him he wanted to come home and was delighted when the Manchester United manager intimated that if he was available he would be bidding.

After a typical Italian complication when Torino attempted to sell him to rivals Juventus for £160,000, Gigi Peronace smoothed the way for him to return to Manchester for a record £115,000 fee with Denis a sadder but probably better player after his year abroad.

Denis had been in a lot of trouble in Italy but he had still

Always quick to retaliate, Denis feared no-one . . . not even his old team-mate Maurice Setters playing in this confrontation for Stoke City.

scored 10 goals in 27 League matches, a creditable effort when you consider that just four more goals would have made him top scorer in the whole of the Italian League.

To say he was glad to be back in English football is an understatement. He was ready to settle down and happy indeed to link up with the manager who had given him his first Scottish cap.

His first season, 1962-63, was an eventful one, in which he was given a striker's role playing alongside David Herd. The team, still rebuilding after Munich, was nearly relegated but showed its potential by winning the F.A. Cup, beating Leicester City 3-1 in the final.

Law remembers it well.

'I can see Paddy Crerand now hitting me with a perfect

ball from the left wing. I turned quickly and shot past Gordon Banks' right hand. It was the first goal, and one I had always dreamed of scoring at Wembley. It was one of the greatest games I played for United.'

Even though United finished 19th in the League, there was nothing wrong with the goal scoring. Denis got 23 goals from 38 League appearances while David Herd scored 19.

Things came together better the following year with Law hitting a fabulous goal-a-game ratio of 30 from 30 appearances. Herd got his usual 20, and with the help of some tighter defence they finished runners-up for the championship.

From there they launched a tremendous campaign to win the championship of 1964-65. There were 28 goals from Law, 20 from Herd, 15 by John Connelly and 10 apiece from Bobby Charlton and the fast-emerging George Best.

They reached the semi-finals of the F.A. Cup three seasons in succession and repeated their championship success in 1966-67. Again Law was top scorer with 23 goals, well backed up by an all-star attack featuring Herd, Charlton and Best.

The title win set them up for another crack at Europe, and this time of course they went all the way, beating Benfica in extra time at Wembley in 1968 to become the first English club to win the European Cup.

Sadly for Denis he missed the final. A long battle with a knee injury ended with admission to hospital three days before the big day at Wembley and the surgeon removed a piece of cartilage more than an inch long.

Some people had thought that Denis was imagining the pain in his knee because no-one had been able to find anything really wrong.

When the offending piece of gristle was located, Denis put it in a bottle and labelled it: 'They said this was in my mind.'

Always the cheeky chappie, especially since hanging up his boots and winning admirers for his perceptive comments on the game on radio and television.

Perhaps because he missed the final, Denis looks to the European Cup of 1965-66 for the highlight of his career in Europe, and he picks out the quarter-final second leg against Benfica in Lisbon as his most joyful experience.

United had beaten the Portuguese 3-2 at Old Trafford in the first leg. The Benfica players had walked off smiling and not many other people considered a one-goal advantage would be enough to see the Reds through in Lisbon.

'Benfica in 1966 were the cream. They had been in three European Cup finals and had taken over from the legendary Real Madrid as top dogs,' explains Denis.

'Two years previously we had been beaten 5-0 in Lisbon in the Cup Winners Cup, and when we went out, all the Portuguese fans were holding their hands with all five fingers up, giving us the salute.

'Sir Matt Busby had made tactical plans for a careful start because we could ill afford to give away an early goal, and see our slender advantage wiped out.

'To say we were keyed up would be an understatement. There was an 80,000 crowd packing the famous Stadium of Light, and I wasn't exactly pleased when Pat Crerand, kicking a ball about in the dressing room, banged it against the mirror.

'The glass shattered, and though no-one said anything, I imagine everyone was thinking about seven years' bad luck. It certainly didn't help the mood, yet we went out and were three goals up in the first quarter of an hour.

'It was incredible and the best performance in my view from a United team in Europe. It was a beautiful experience and a joy to share in that splendid team effort.

'George Best, only 19 at the time, grabbed the headlines and no-one begrudged him that; after all it was cheeky George who scored the first two goals and helped lay on the third for John Connelly.

'In the last quarter of an hour I put Pat Crerand in for a goal and Bobby Charlton waltzed through for the fifth.

'My name was missing from the scoresheet, but it was of no consequence because I knew I had played well, just like everyone else in the team.

'It was unusual for the three so-called stars, Charlton, Law and Best, all to turn it on in the same match, but we did that night. So did Nobby Stiles, Pat Crerand, John Connelly and the rest of them.

'Everything came off for us. By rights we should have

Denis Law was at his scoring peak with 28 goals to help win the League championship in season 1964-65, Manchester United's first title success after Munich. The team lined up:
Back row: Nobby Stiles, Tony Dunne, David Gaskell, Pat Dunne, Pat Crerand, John Fitzpatrick.
Middle: Jack Crompton (trainer), Shay Brennan, David Sadler, Bill Foulkes, John Aston, Noel Cantwell, Matt Busby (manager).
Front: John Connelly, Bobby Charlton, David Herd, Denis Law, George Best.

gone on to win the European Cup that year, but we played badly in the semi-final against Partizan Belgrade, losing 2-0 in Yugoslavia and winning only 1-0 back at Old Trafford.

'So we missed out on final glory. But Sir Matt Busby called our performance in Lisbon "our finest hour" and I think he summed it up well.'

After recovering from his knee operation Denis came back to make 30 League appearances in season 1968-69 and score 14 goals, but George Best had taken over now as the major goal scorer.

Traumatic times also lay ahead as first Wilf McGuinness and then Frank O'Farrell took over as manager, trying to follow in the famous footsteps of Sir Matt Busby.

Denis was still worth his place, but his best years were over and when Tommy Docherty breezed in he greatly upset the Lawman by giving him a free transfer at the end of season 1972-73 after promising that there would be a job on the staff for him.

The manner of the public announcement also riled the player who thought it had been agreed that his retirement should wait until his testimonial the following season. Instead to his horror he was home in Aberdeen when his picture was flashed on the television screen with the news that United had given him a free.

So that summer he moved back across the road for a final season with Manchester City which ended with the bizarre situation of scoring a goal which looked at the time to have sent United down to the Second Division.

In fact United would have gone down anyway because their rivals in distress both won their games, but Denis wasn't to know that after almost casually back-heeling the ball past Alex Stepney for the only goal of the game. He walked back to the centre circle looking like a man who had just accidentally stabbed his best friend in the back!

Law's nine goals in 24 League appearances that season at Maine Road earned him a place in the 1974 Scottish World Cup squad for Germany, and he played in their opening group game against Zaire.

Scotland won 2-0, but Denis was then dropped in favour of Willie Morgan. He had played his last major game, and when he discovered at the start of the following season that Tony Book didn't have a first-team place for him, he retired.

It had been a stormy career at times with his aggression and short fuse always liable to see him in conflict with referees. He also seemed to have a knack of needling officialdom who twice suspended him for 28-day periods, draconian punishment for a player whose main offence was one of retaliation; the squint-eyed little boy was still always ready to fight.

But the good times far outweighed the bad. Although

his disciplinary record prevented him ever being voted Footballer of the Year by the English soccer writers, their Continental counterparts more readily appreciated pure talent and they voted him European Footballer of the Year in 1964, a well deserved recognition.

Denis looks back fondly on his 11 seasons with Manchester United.

'It was the Swinging Sixties in soccer as well as in the entertainment world with the Beatles, and I think we saw football at its best in that period.

'I was privileged to play in a great side. It was a beautiful team to play in with players like Pat Crerand, Bobby Charlton, Nobby Stiles, and George Best coming along. Over a period of five years it was a joy for the entertainment and goals.

'We always felt that if the opposition scored one, we could score two, and if they got two we could score three. It didn't always work out that way, but that was the feeling, and it was all very special for me.'

Sir Matt fretted about his fiery nature but doesn't hesitate to put him in his team of all-time greats.

He says: 'Denis Law was the most expensive signing I ever made, but on achievement he turned out to be the cheapest. The Italians dragged me and my chairman all over Europe before we were able to complete the signing, and at one time I was so angry at the way we were being treated that I almost pulled out of the deal.

'I'm extremely glad that I didn't. Once we had got Denis to Old Trafford I knew that we had the most exciting player in the game. He was the quickest-thinking player I ever saw, seconds quicker than anyone else. He had the most tremendous acceleration, and could leap to enormous heights to head the ball with almost unbelievable accuracy, and often with the power of a shot.

'He had the courage to take on the biggest and most ferocious opponents, and his passing was impeccable. He was one of the most unselfish players I have ever seen. If he was not in the best position to score he would give the ball to someone who was.

'When a chance was on for him, even only a half-chance, or in some cases no chance at all for anybody else but him, whether he had his back to goal, was sideways on, or the ball was on the deck or up at shoulder height, he would have it in the net with such power and acrobatic agility that colleagues and opponents alike could only stand and gasp.

'No other player scored as many miracle goals as Denis Law. Goals which looked simple as Denis tapped them in were simple only because Denis got himself into position so quickly that opponents just could not cope with him.

'He was the first British player to salute the crowd. Early on at Old Trafford the multitudes cheered him and he soon became what the crowd called him . . . The King.'

Sir Matt adds: 'He is a good friend and a warm-hearted family man who is never less than cheerful.'

Manchester is still home to Denis and his wife Diane with their five children. He works for a printing company, but is a familiar voice on radio and television with comments on football as perceptive and sharp as he was in opposition goalmouths.

DENIS LAW'S RECORD

	LEAGUE		F.A. CUP		F.L. CUP		EUROPE		TOTAL	
	App	Gls	App	Gls	App	Gls	App	Gls	App	Gls
1962-63	38	23	6	6					44	29
1963-64	30	30	6	10			5	6	41	46
1964-65	36	28	6	3			10	8	52	39
1965-66	33	15	7	6			8	3	48	24
1966-67	36	23	2	2					38	25
1967-68	23	7	1				3	2	27	9
1968-69	30	14	6	7			7	9	43	30
1969-70	10/1	2	/2		3	1			13/3	3
1970-71	28	15	2		4	1			34	16
1971-72	32/1	13	7		2				41/1	13
1972-73	9/2	1	1		2	1			12/2	2
	305/4	171	44/2	34	11	3	33	28	393/6	236

SCOTLAND: 1962 v Wales, Northern Ireland; 1963 v England, Austria, Norway, Republic of Ireland, Spain, Norway, Wales; 1964 v England, West Germany, Wales, Finland, Northern Ireland; 1965 v England, Spain, Poland, Finland, Northern Ireland, Poland; 1966 v England, Wales; 1967 v England, USSR, Northern Ireland; 1968 v Austria; 1969 v West Germany, Northern Ireland; 1972 v Peru, Northern Ireland, Wales, England, Yugoslavia, Czechoslovakia, Brazil (35 Caps).

CHAPTER EIGHT

George Best

Slack Alice got her man early.

George Best was only 26 when he turned his back on serious football to open a night club in Manchester with the appropriate name of Slack Alice.

For it was undoubtedly the fatal combination of birds and booze which extinguished the flame of genius which had brought a new dimension to the game of football.

Many bemoan what they consider to be a premature departure from the stage, even people like the scruffy, stubbly night porter who took a slightly worse-for-wear George up in the lift to his hotel bedroom in the early hours of one morning in London.

He fixed his rheumy old eyes on the wayward Irishman and delivered his judgment: 'What a terrible waste your life has been.' George, with a mindful of memories and a glance at Miss World on his arm, smiled.

And with good cause, because if he had been of a different temperament and had wanted to, there is no doubt that George Best was young enough at 26 to have gone on for much longer than he did. It would have been nice for the rest of us if he had continued to grace the game with his unparalleled talent for another few more years.

It must have been particularly frustrating for Frank O'Farrell, the luckless manager who had to suffer the break-up of Best's career and didn't know whether the player was with him or on his way.

But every man has the right to choose his life, and what the game too often forgets is that George Best played for 11 seasons in the First Division for Manchester United.

George Best . . . a cult figure who became the James Dean of football, but always a magical player.

He might have finished as something of a wandering star, but he was hardly a passing stranger. His career was one of substance and of course marvellous achievement.

So while fans at the time might have concluded that he was needlessly throwing away a great career, he had in fact packed more into his football life than the majority of professional players.

He perhaps walked out young, but people forget he

started young, and by the time he quit at Old Trafford he had played 466 League, Cup and European games and scored 178 goals.

The other significant factor is that once he had established himself in the side he rarely missed a game. In fact in six of his seasons he made either 40, 41 or a full-house 42 appearances.

That's hardly the career of a fly-by-night; and when you consider how often he turned on the magic, he was entitled to call it a day when it suited him. George Best more than paid his dues, he transported a great many people to the heights of delight . . . and I'm not even including the girls who flocked to worship his good looks and swoon at the feet of a cult figure who took soccer into the Swinging Sixties.

George Best was football's answer to the Beatles, and indeed after one particularly astonishing performance in Lisbon the Portuguese Press hailed him as El Beatle. He was only 19 and he had virtually beaten Benfica on his own.

Off the field he was the Carnaby Street kid on the brink of opening a boutique. A trendy dresser himself with his Beatle haircut, never again would the typical footballer have short back and sides with a pub the most to look forward to when he hung up his boots!

A star was born that night in the Stadium of Light which was to shine so brightly in the most successful period of Manchester United's history.

But like Denis Law before him, few who saw George arrive in Manchester from Belfast would have guessed what lay ahead. For he was another scrap of a lad who looked too frail for football.

He hadn't made the Irish schoolboy team because he wasn't strong or big enough, but Bob Bishop, United's Northern Ireland scout, was a better judge, and after watching him play for Cregagh Boys Club he signed him up for Old Trafford.

Mrs Mary Fullaway, his landlady at his Chorlton digs, says: 'He looked more like a little jockey than a footballer. He was puny and petrified.'

The Swinging Sixties saw George Best emerge as a boutique owner always prepared to sport a trendy fashion himself.

He was also homesick and just 24 hours after his arrival, he and Eric McMordie, a boy who had also been signed from Belfast, caught the *Ulster Prince* night ferry back home to Belfast.

Fortunately the alarm was soon raised at Old Trafford and Matt Busby got in touch with Mr Best who promised to send the youngsters back on the understanding that United would find his son a job in case football didn't work out.

Chief scout Joe Armstrong secured him an office job because he had beautiful handwriting, and he worked in the afternoons for the Manchester Ship Canal Company.

That didn't last long, though, because whatever the player's shortcomings, he always loved training. Even when his disappearing acts started, no-one complained about his appetite for playing once he was out on a pitch.

One of the first to appreciate his nimble-footed dribbling ability was Harry Gregg who volunteered to play in an impromptu five-a-side game with the youngsters at The Cliff training ground one afternoon.

One of the boys, the skinny one, had brought the ball up to him and sent him diving the wrong way as he tapped the ball into the other end of the net.

Any kid can be lucky the first time, thought Harry, but this titch of a youngster did it a second time. United's Irish international goalkeeper was never a player to enjoy looking foolish so you can be sure he was trying.

Says Harry: 'I had always prided myself on the fact that I could make forwards do what I wanted in those kind of circumstances, but this slip of a boy just shook his hips and had me diving at fresh air. I knew in that moment that the club had a very rare talent on their hands.

'What happened to George Best later is another story, and I make no judgment on his lifestyle. But I will say this: In all the years I have known him he has always listened to any advice I have given him, and he, more than any one player, brought the European Cup to Old Trafford.

'I would say that United started to become a great side again when they signed Denis Law. It is also impossible to overstate the contribution Bobby Charlton made over the years.

'But George Best was a genius. At his peak he was at least the equal of any player in the world . . . and probably the best.'

The Irishman was not slow to acquire the trapping of success with the kind of sports car made to measure for a young man about town.

United have won the F.A. Youth Cup only once since the Munich accident, and significantly that was in season 1963-64 when Best was in the side along with the likes of David Sadler, who lived in the same digs, John Aston, John Fitzpatrick, Bobby Noble and Jimmy Rimmer.

That same season at the age of 17 and four months he was given his League debut with only a handful of reserve outings behind him. He played at outside right against Graham Williams, a fierce-tackling Welsh international, and came through well.

His debut team on 14 September, 1963, lined up: Gregg, Dunne, Cantwell, Crerand, Foulkes, Setters, Best, Stiles, Sadler, Chisnall, Charlton.

He went back into the reserves until Christmas and a humiliating 6-1 defeat against Burnley at Turf Moor. Out of the side went the two wingers, Shay Brennan and Albert Quixall; at the same time a telegram was sent to Belfast, where Best was on holiday, recalling him to Old Trafford.

With Best and Willie Anderson on the flanks, two days

later, the Reds swept to a revengeful 5-1 victory with Best one of the scorers.

I remember asking him on the morning of the match if he was excited to be playing after so few reserve matches. The only response I got from him was a shrug of the shoulders and a flat 'No'. He wasn't kidding either. Right through his career he was always one of the last to get changed for action. He would often stand chatting to friends until half an hour before kick-off while most of his team-mates were already stripped and feeling the tension.

George stayed in the side until the end of the season, scoring three goals in a total of 17 League appearances. He also enjoyed a run in the F.A. Cup to reach the semi-finals, contributing a couple of goals and finally attracting the attention of the Northern Ireland selectors who had passed him over as a schoolboy.

They weren't going to delay this time, and after just 21 first-team games, Ireland gave him his first Irish cap, playing at outside right against Wales at Swansea in April, 1964.

He went on to make a total of 32 appearances for his country, but was never able to make quite the same mark for Ireland. Too often he seemed to be injured for internationals, or he was required for a club commitment. It was not a particularly good era for Irish football in the days of Best either, and as we saw with United towards the end of his career, George was never at his best in a struggling side.

Certainly he couldn't complain about the players around him at Old Trafford when he arrived on the scene.

Matt Busby had been steadily building after Munich, and after bringing John Connelly, Denis Law and Pat Crerand to Old Trafford to augment the players beginning to roll off his own production line, he had a team again. Best broke through to put the icing on the cake and in his first full season he helped to win the League championship, United's first title success after Munich.

George missed only one game and scored 10 goals,

Once on the football field he could dribble round opponents as if the ball was tied to his bootlaces.

which for a newcomer was a fabulous effort. Denis Law was at the peak of his considerable powers and scored 28, backed up by 20 from David Herd, 15 from John Connelly and 10 by Bobby Charlton. It was an all-action forward line and the fans went wild because it was an achievement that many people thought would be impossible so soon after the destruction of the Busby Babes.

Best represented the new wave of glory and appropriately enough scored the first goal in a 3-1 victory over Arsenal which saw the Reds clinch the title on goal average from Leeds United.

The champions were: Pat Dunne, Brennan, Tony Dunne,

Crerand, Foulkes, Stiles, Connelly, Charlton, Herd, Law, Best.

The championship naturally brought a return to the European Cup for the first time since the fateful trip to Belgrade in 1958, and though George had figured in both the European Cup Winners Cup and the Fairs Cup in the previous two seasons, everyone regarded the championship of the champions as the real thing.

The Reds eased through against Helsinki and Vorwaerts, the East German army team, to meet Benfica in the quarter-finals, and launch George Best as a world star.

This was the tie that saw George come home from Lisbon as El Beatle.

The Reds had taken a narrow 3-2 lead to Portugal from the first leg and the home fans were in confident mood as they greeted the teams with a barrage of multi-coloured rockets and a tumultuous roar.

United's tactics were simply to play safe and hold their opponents for the first 20 minutes, but by that time Best had scored twice and so had John Connelly.

George got the first after only six minutes when Bobby Charlton was brought down and Tony Dunne floated the free kick goalwards for the Irish imp to nod the ball past Costa Pereira.

In the 12th minute Harry Gregg punted the ball towards the halfway line. David Herd flicked it on with a header for Best to weave past three stunned defenders all on his own and finish with a goal which was sensational by any standards.

United closed with a 5-1 win on the night for an aggregate 8-3 victory. It was audacious, it was superb and it established George Best with a world ranking.

'He must have had cotton wool in his ears when we made our plans,' said a delighted Busby.

George described the moment in his book: 'I felt superb. The atmosphere sent the blood coursing through my veins, adding power to my muscles, imagination to my brain.'

Anything went as the juggler left opponents dazed by his skill.

He didn't feel quite so assured when a man rushed up to him as he left the field brandishing a knife; all ended well, though, when he realised that all the fan wanted was to hack off a lock of the Beatle hair to keep as a memento of a great occasion!

United were immediately installed as favourites to go the whole way and become champions of Europe, but fate had a cruel trick to play. The hero of Lisbon twisted his knee in a tackle in an F.A. Cup tie against Preston a fortnight later.

United left him out of the next couple of games and then strapped him up for the first leg of the European semi-final against Partizan Belgrade in Yugoslavia. United lost 2-0.

Certainly Best did not repeat his Lisbon extravaganza, but he still looked their most dangerous forward.

But the game was the last of the season for Best who came straight home for a cartilage operation. The team won the second leg 1-0, not enough to undo the damage in Belgrade. Three days later they went out of the F.A. Cup as well in another semi-final defeat, losing 1-0 to Everton at Burnden Park.

It seemed that when Best dropped out, the magic went as well.

In the League the Reds finished fourth after concentrating most of their efforts on Cup football.

But they were a good side and the following season, 1966-67, without any European involvement and knocked out of the F.A. Cup as early as the fourth round with a similarly early exit in the League Cup, they focused on the championship again — and won it.

George was an ever-present and scored 10 goals in a campaign which saw them finish at the top, four points in front of Nottingham Forest.

Everything was coming together for the Irishman now as United launched into their season of destiny in 1967-68. It was the year of their European Cup triumph and they finished runners-up in the League.

Significantly it was also George Best's peak season, and a year which proved to be the watershed of his career.

He enjoyed his best-ever scoring season with 28 League goals from 41 appearances, overshadowing Denis Law for the first time. It looked at one stage as if the Reds would pull off a League and European Cup double, but towards the end the demands of Europe saw them lose a five-point lead and finish two points behind Manchester City.

Best was an inspiration along the European trail, especially when they came up against the mighty Real Madrid in the semi-finals. It was the Irishman who scored at Old Trafford to give the Reds a slender 1-0 lead to take to Spain.

It hardly seemed enough and things certainly looked

George's ability attracted a lot of fierce tackling, but he never shied away and in fact loved to invite a challenge.

black when they went in at half-time 3-1 down on the night. Matt Busby hammered home the fact that the aggregate score was 3-2, so all was not lost, and his players responded.

David Sadler shot the aggregate equaliser to set the stage for one of the most remarkable goals in United's European history.

George went on a long searing sprint down the right flank from a throw-in, leaving Sanchis and Zoco trailing in his wake. Ninety-nine times out of a hundred in situations like that, the highly individualistic Best would have cut in and gone for it.

This time, though, he rolled a pass back for Bill Foulkes, of all players, to turn the ball into a corner of the goal. United's granite centre half hardly ever left his defensive lines, and certainly it must have been the first time in his career that George Best had passed to him in the opposition penalty area.

What a winner and an inspiration for their final against Benfica at Wembley; and again it was George Best tipping the balance at the decisive moment.

Normal time had ended with the score level at 1-1. Then in the first minute of extra time, Brian Kidd headed Alex Stepney's goal kick on for Best to chase.

Watch-dog Cruz was tiring as George tore away to take the ball round the advancing Henrique in a wide curve and clip it cleanly into the empty net.

It was the killer goal as United went on to their final convincing scoreline of 4-1 to give Matt Busby his dream European Cup.

Best's contribution had been widely noted. Almost inevitably he was chosen Player of the Year in Northern Ireland. The English football writers gave him their award as well, and six months later he was voted European Footballer of the Year, the youngest ever.

The following season, 1968-69, saw George do his stuff with 19 League goals from 41 appearances, and United reached the semi-finals of the European Cup defending their title.

But support for George was waning; cracks were appearing. The team sagged to 11th in the League as the club headed for a period of change.

Sir Matt Busby retired to make way for Wilf McGuinness, and then Frank O'Farrell took over. The management changes didn't suit the Best temperament, and suddenly from being a match winner and a hero he became a headache.

His restless spirit brought him into conflict with referees

He had his fair share of trouble with referees, though, despite the efforts of Nobby Stiles to drag him away from this clash.

and into all manner of scrapes off the field, with pretty, nay gorgeous, girls never far away.

Season 1969-70 saw him twice sent off, the first time for knocking the ball out of referee Jack Taylor's hands, and the second when he was playing for Ireland against Scotland he was reported for throwing mud and spitting at referee Eric Jennings.

He was suspended for a month for the first offence and escaped punishment for the second thanks to the Irish F.A.

He still managed to score 15 goals to help the team into eighth place. Indeed he scored 18 goals in each of his next two seasons as well, and only missed four games.

He was becoming increasingly difficult to manage, though. For instance he failed to turn up for training on Christmas Day, 1970, the only player to shirk an obviously unpopular chore.

Wilf McGuinness was in a dilemma. First it was decided to send him back home when he reported for the next day's match at Derby County. Then came second thoughts; they let him play but fined him £50; of course he scored to help achieve a 4-4 draw, but should expediency have come before club discipline?

Wilf was in a similar pickle when he caught George in his hotel bedroom with a girl just a couple of hours before an F.A. Cup semi-final. The situation called for disciplinary action, but how do you leave your best player out of the team?

Frank O'Farrell inherited a major problem with the still popular Irishman's life fast getting out of control.

In 1971 he was suspended for a fortnight after missing training and failing to report for a match. He also received a suspended six-week ban from the F.A. after being cautioned three times by referees.

He was sent off against Chelsea for swearing at the referee, later cleared when Willie Morgan claimed that the abuse had been directed at him. He pulled out of an international after threats on his life, said to have been made by the IRA.

The year 1972 was the beginning of the end when in January he walked out and missed a week's training. United sent him back to his old digs in Chorlton.

In May he skipped United's end of season trip to Israel and turned up instead on the Costa del Sol where he held Press conferences, claiming that he was drinking a bottle of vodka a day.

'Mentally and physically I am a bloody wreck,' he declared.

He changed his mind after 17 days in retirement, and pre-season he was suspended for two weeks by United and told to live with Pat Crerand. He was sent off playing for Ireland and in November failed to turn up for training again. United fined and dropped him.

Just before Christmas, 1972, United sacked Frank O'Farrell and at the same time issued a statement saying that George Best would remain on the transfer list and would not be selected again for Manchester United.

Their announcement crossed with a letter from the player announcing his retirement.

It was a sad end to a glorious career. He later played for Hibs, Dunstable, Stockport County, Fulham and in America where he did well for a period.

George pinpoints the start of his troubles to the European Cup triumph, and says: 'It was almost as if the established people at the club — the players as well as backroom staff — thought that winning the European Cup was the ultimate achievement.

'They were happy to relax and rest on their laurels. But to me, with a whole career ahead of me, it looked as if the future contained nothing but grafting about in the middle of the table, losing as many games as we won.'

He certainly left Old Trafford on a sour note. His former team-mate Willie Morgan, who had once rescued him from suspension, pulled no punches when he said: 'George thought he was the James Bond of soccer.

'He had everything he wanted and he pleased himself. He had money, girls and tremendous publicity. He lived from day to day. Until right to the end, he got away with it when he missed training or ran away. So he didn't care. People made excuses for him; he didn't even have to bother to make them himself.

'People talk about pressures and depressions. It was rubbish. He just hadn't any responsibilities, nothing to worry about at all.

'All kinds of people covered up for him, even the Press, and he was lucky to get away with it for so long.'

More sympathetically, Bill Foulkes recalls: 'Looking back I feel guilty. George was a youngster when he came into a great side, and I don't think we senior players took enough interest in him.

'Older players influenced me a great deal when I was young, but we failed to influence George Best. We all went our separate ways and I wish now we had involved him more away from the ground.'

At the time of writing he has had a testimonial match in Belfast, he plays the occasional match and he runs a night-club in London. He has a son Calum Milan Best.

A lot of us feared for his future when he left Manchester, and the demon drink seems to have been an ongoing problem for him.

But it's clear that George Best is a survivor as well as living in my thoughts and in the memories of thousands of folk as an unsurpassed prince of players.

The sight of his slim figure weaving its way through a pack of desperate defenders with the ball seemingly tied to his boots was poetry. He had uncanny balance which meant that not only was he able to ride tackles, he could challenge for possession himself and pluck the ball away from an opponent without even knocking him over.

He is the only player I have ever seen who could play a one-two off an opponent's legs.

Forget Slack Alice . . . the fans had the best of George Best out on the pitch!

GEORGE BEST'S RECORD

	LEAGUE		F.A. CUP		F.L. CUP		EUROPE		TOTAL	
	App	Gls	App	Gls	App	Gls	App	Gls	App	Gls
1963-64	17	4	7	2			2		26	6
1964-65	41	10	7	2			11	2	59	14
1965-66	31	9	5	3			6	4	42	16
1966-67	42	10	2		1				45	10
1967-68	41	28	2	1			9	3	52	32
1968-69	41	19	6	1			6	2	53	22
1969-70	37	15	8	6	8	2			53	23
1970-71	40	18	2	1	6	2			48	21
1971-72	40	18	7	5	6	3			53	26
1972-73	19	4			4	2			23	6
1973-74	12	2							12	2
	361	137	46	21	25	9	34	11	466	178

NORTHERN IRELAND: 1964 v Wales, Uruguay, England, Switzerland (twice), Scotland; 1965 v Holland (twice), Albania, Scotland, England, Albania; 1966 v England; 1967 v Scotland; 1968 v Turkey; 1969 v England, Scotland, Wales, USSR; 1970 v Scotland, England, Wales, Spain; 1971 v Cyprus (twice), England, Scotland, Wales, USSR; 1972 v Spain, Bulgaria; 1973 v Portugal (32 Caps).

CHAPTER NINE

Nobby Stiles

Who will ever forget the jig of joy danced round Wembley by little Nobby Stiles after England had won the World Cup of 1966?

With his socks rolled round his ankles and an ear-splitting grin revealing the absence of front teeth, Nobby cavorted his way into the affections of fans who knew they had just seen a footballer who had played his heart out for his country.

That was the only way he knew to play, of course, and while never the most elegant or graceful of players, he was a brilliant reader of the game as a defender and he was a key member of Manchester United's teams through the Sixties.

Every team needs a Nobby Stiles. They rarely get the credit they deserve, but Matt Busby valued Nobby enormously, and so did Alf Ramsey when he consistently selected him to knit together the more highly tuned thoroughbreds of his successful England team.

Nobby was a winner of the ball and a provider, as well as showing an amazing knack for spotting danger posed by the opposition. Bobby Charlton once told me that his pal reminded him of a sheep dog constantly rounding up the sheep which got out of line and putting them firmly back in the pen.

Of course he snapped at a few heels to do it, and he had a reputation for strong tackling and fierce aggression.

The fans abroad certainly hated him. In his career of 14 years at Old Trafford he was hit on the head by a bottle in Madrid, hissed and spat at in Italy and called an assassin in South America.

Nobby Stiles, looking less like El Bandido nowadays, meets up again with Sir Matt Busby with a toast perhaps to happy memories.

He could be clumsy, both on and off the field. He frequently left an accidental trail of destruction in team hotels. He once looked at the sturdy oak panelling and solid carved mantelpiece and said how much he admired its strength and the fact that it had obviously been there for years. He slapped it with his hand to emphasise the point, and a piece came away.

Nothing was safe when Nobby was around.

Of course bad eyesight didn't help a natural tendency to be clumsy, especially before he got his contact lenses. His team-mates swear that at one after-match banquet Nobby left the room and was away ages; they say that he went back into another reception and had actually sat down chatting before realising he was with a different lot of people!

A great many of his awkward-looking tackles were probably because without his spectacles he simply couldn't see properly; certainly his tackling improved after he was fitted with contact lenses.

That didn't stop one intrepid reporter suggesting that he played as if he was trying to create orders for his father's business as an undertaker.

He hailed from Manchester's richly productive football area of Collyhurst, and after winning five England schoolboy caps he signed for the Reds as an apprentice. His League debut came in October, 1960, at the age of 18 in a drawn game at Bolton and he stayed in the side for the rest of a rather undistinguished season.

The team finished seventh as the effects of Munich bit home, and indeed he had a difficult apprenticeship in the first team — they were 15th and then 19th in the following seasons — before Matt Busby could create his successful side of the mid-Sixties.

Stiles shared in the F.A. Cup run of 1963 though he didn't play in the final. Maurice Setters frequently kept him out of the team, but in season 1964-65 he missed only one League match on the way to winning the championship and he had settled into his best position alongside Bill Foulkes in defence.

Crerand, Foulkes and Stiles was the halfback line which prospered to win the League title again in 1966-67 and Stiles hardly missed a match.

By this time Alf Ramsey was playing him as his midfield tiger in front of the central defenders Jack Charlton and Bobby Moore. He wore the number four shirt right through the World Cup triumph in 1966, but not without a fright that he might lose his place following a controversial challenge in the group game against France on Jacques Simon.

His tackle was a fraction late and looked awful. The Frenchman lay very still and even Nobby thought he had hurt him badly.

He recalls: 'Everyone said my tackle was filthy. Danny Blanchflower on television said he was embarrassed, though he had never liked my style of play from the first

This was the more familiar image of Nobby Stiles during his playing days with fangs at the ready!

time I played against him as an 18-year-old. He thought everyone should play his style and I hustled him. He never liked me after that.

'The tackle which put Simon down made me feel sick until he got up again, but the ball was there when I went in. I never followed through late. I didn't chop the player down and I never put the boot in. It upset me to see him on the ground.

'After the match I sat in the dressing room with my head in my hands and asked the trainers: "Is there something wrong with me? Am I getting too hard?"

'FIFA cautioned me for a late tackle and that's when all the publicity blew up. The quarter-final against Argentina was the next game and if Alf Ramsey had left me out I would have understood. In fact I was half expecting it.

'But the manager sorted me out, got me out of the dumps and made me feel absolutely sky-high. He told me he didn't feel I had been dirty, and that was important to me. He told me not to worry about what people were saying. He said just get the ball and play it, nice and simple all the time, and to stop trying to do a bit more with it just because some folk were howling for Nobby Stiles to be more creative.

'Alf made me believe in myself again and I didn't feel a culprit any more.'

England had opened the finals with a goalless draw against Uruguay and then beaten Mexico and France, both by 2-0, to finish top of their group and put them in the last eight against Argentina.

Ramsey kept faith with Stiles, despite a great deal of clamour for him to be dropped. As it turned out, the game found a new villain when Rattin, the Argentinian captain, was ordered off following a fairly innocuous tackle on Bobby Charlton and then later in the game for protesting to the referee about the booking of one of his men.

England won with a late header by Geoff Hurst. Stiles had played impeccably and he had another great game in the semi-final when Bobby Charlton scored twice in a 2-1 victory over a sporting Portuguese side.

Stiles made his mark as a world-class player with his astute covering, especially against the dangerous Eusebio.

Nobby, in action here against Watford, was a great reader of the game as well as a fierce ball-winner.

There was never any doubt by then that Nobby would play in the final against Germany. England won 4-2 in extra time after Germany had levelled the game to 2-2 in the final minute of normal play.

The equaliser had come as a sickening blow to English hopes and it was then that they really drew on the resilience of spirited players like Nobby Stiles and Alan Ball.

It was Stiles who released the ball to Ball on the wing

which led to England's third goal which was the beginning of the end for the Germans. Ball crossed for Hurst to head against the bar. The ball bounced down and after an agonising wait and consultation with the Russian linesman, the Swiss referee, Gottfried Dienst, ruled that it had crossed the line and was a goal.

Hurst completed his hat-trick and Stiles and George Cohen collapsed in tearful embrace on the ground. Soon they were back on their feet and Nobby went on his lap of honour to win the hearts of the fans all over again.

For him it was a double celebration. Not only was he a World Cup winner . . . but the world loved him as well.

As Nobby put it at the time: 'A weedy-looking, short-sighted bloke with a top plate of false teeth may not be everyone's idea of a sporting hero . . . but I feel a hero.

'I've been made one by the World Cup and I think my little dance round Wembley at the end with the telly showing me without my bridgework baring my two fangs made folk like me.

'Up till then I got poison pen letters and insults in the street. Nut-cases wanted to fill me in. I got a letter once addressed "Dear Ugly, Don't look round when you come down the tunnel on Saturday because you might get a hatchet in your head."

'The World Cup changed all that, though I have got to say I never thought I was a villain myself. I'm not all that hard a man on the field; maybe little fellows just get narky a bit quicker.

'After all my nickname with the England and Manchester United players was always "Happy".'

The World Cup gave Nobby a new stature in the game and it showed on his return to domestic football and the championship success of 1966-67 which saw the Reds launched into the European Cup to give Nobby the rare double of winners' medals as a champion for both club and country.

Again Nobby found himself up against Eusebio when the Reds met Benfica in the final. It was their fourth

The will to win was always very evident, even if it meant a finger-wagging and a few home truths for goalkeeper Alex Stepney, his own team-mate.

meeting and United's 4-1 victory at Wembley in extra time came to a close with Eusebio still without a goal against the Reds save for a penalty.

The final must have given Nobby a feeling of *déja vu* when Benfica equalised 10 minutes from the end of normal time.

'If the game had had another 10 minutes to go without a break I think we would have lost,' he explained. 'There we were, on top and in front, but when they scored it knocked the heart out of us.

'We suddenly realised how tired we were. For me it was like the World Cup all over again when Germany pulled level just before the end.'

Also like the World Cup, United's players pulled out something extra with three goals in extra time to win handsomely, and the fact that Nobby Stiles was in both teams is, I'm sure, a significant factor.

Nobby's career and standing in the game was obviously at a peak, but his bad boy image still cast a shadow, as he discovered when United played Estudiantes, the champions of South America, for the world club championship early in the following season.

The first leg was played in Buenos Aires and as far as the Argentinians were concerned Nobby Stiles was El Bandido. They remembered Nobby from the World Cup final and had nursed a sense of injustice against the English following Sir Alf Ramsey's reference to their team playing like 'animals'.

Nobby remembers: 'It was a different world in South America. Before the kick-off there were gaily dressed folk dancers performing in front of steel-helmeted riot police armed with tear gas guns.

'It was quite incongruous, and the atmosphere was highly charged when we walked out with clouds of red smoke billowing from a bomb someone had let off.

'I suppose even before the game had started I was regarded as the villain of the piece. I knew I always had a reputation as a fairly aggressive player, but the South American Press had really gone to town.

Nobby Stiles found a friend in Sir Alf Ramsey as the England manager stood by him to win the World Cup of 1966.

'They called me an assassin, and even in the match programme I was described as "brutal, badly intentioned and a bad sportsman".

'I could hardly expect the home fans to be on my side after that — and they weren't and I think the referee must have read the programme as well. I certainly didn't get much sympathy from him.'

Nobby's particular problem was a wild young man called Carlos Bilardo who surfaced again in 1986 as the manager who guided Argentina to their World Cup triumph in Mexico.

Not many players can claim to have been 'nutted' by a national team manager, but that's what happened when Bilardo was the hatchet man for Estudiantes.

The opening leg in Buenos Aires was a bloody affair all round with Bilardo scarcely hiding the fact that he was out to get Stiles. The confrontation came to a climax when he simply smashed the United man in the face with his head, though it was the insult he added to the injury which really upset Nobby.

'The head butt was bad enough, but then Bilardo threw himself down as if it was me who had hit him. I thought the referee was going to send me off, but I was able to point to the blood running from my cut eye and it made him change his mind,' explained Nobby.

'In actual fact I was sent off later in the match and I was pig sick. Paddy Crerand and I had talked at half-time about how we should try and beat the offside trap they were working. We agreed that if our forwards came out with their defence, then I should make some deep runs through and catch them off guard.

'I thought we had worked it, but the linesman signalled I was offside. I didn't think I was and I just threw my hands in the air. The referee sent me off for dissent.

'It was a bit silly and I was very upset because I thought I had let the side down. There was a lot going on in that game and it seemed ridiculous that I should be sent off for waving my arm.

'Mind you, the referee was a funny chap. He was smoking a cigarette when we all came down the tunnel to go out on the pitch. A lot of people smoke but you don't expect to see the ref having a puff like that!

'We lost 1-0, but the game did have its lighter moments. I remember coming out of the stadium after the match. It was dark and shadowy when I suddenly felt something thrust into my back and a voice whispering into my ear: "Now then El Bandido".

'I thought my end had come — until I realised it was Brian Kidd!

'I missed the return leg in Manchester, suspended because of the sending-off. Estudiantes weren't as bad at Old Trafford, though there were two players sent off, George Best and Hugo Medina after George had retaliated.

'But we weren't at our best. We conceded a goal after five minutes and it killed us. Willie Morgan scored near the end to make it 1-1 on the night, but of course we lost on aggregate with the 1-0 defeat in Buenos Aires.'

Sir Matt Busby felt Nobby had had a raw deal in South America. 'They crucified him and the build-up in the Argentine Press was quite disgraceful,' he said.

Everyone remembers the drama of the Estudiantes match, and of course the achievement of winning the European Cup, but as far as Nobby Stiles is concerned, his favourite run in European competition came in the Inter Cities Fairs Cup of 1965.

It's probably United's least remembered campaign in Europe, but Nobby considers it a highspot of his career.

He explained: 'People recall our European Cup win and the famous encounters with teams like Real Madrid and Benfica, but in my time at Old Trafford we were at our peak when we reached the semi-finals of the Fairs Cup in season 1964-65.

'We played some cracking football and scored five or six goals in nearly every round, sometimes even away from home.

'We opened cautiously enough with a 1-1 draw against

Djurgardens in Sweden but we demolished them 6-1 in the return with the help of a hat-trick from Denis Law.

'We went to Germany and won 6-1 in the first leg against Borussia Dortmund, this time with a hat-trick from Bobby Charlton. For good measure we saw them off 4-0 at Old Trafford.

'The next round pitted us against Everton, which was a shame and understandably the scores were tighter, 1-1 at Old Trafford with a 2-1 win for us at Goodison.

'There seemed to be no stopping us when we went to France and beat Strasbourg 5-0. The home return was goalless, but we had certainly scored some goals overall and we were very confident about the semi-final against Ferencvaros.

'The only doubt in our minds was the fact that it had been an extremely long season.

'We didn't even play Strasbourg until a fortnight after the end of the League season, and it was June before we tackled Ferencvaros.

'It had been a busy season and I know I had played 66 games if you include England Under-23 appearances. We had reached the semi-finals of the F.A. Cup, losing 1-0 to Leeds United in a replay.

'We were also champions after a run of 10 wins in 11 matches, but the long, tiring season was perhaps beginning to have an effect, and we didn't play particularly well in the first leg against the Hungarians.

'Denis Law scored a penalty, and though a fellow called Novak put Ferencvaros level, we seemed to be OK after two goals by David Herd to lead 3-1.

'Then we gave away a silly goal, Pat Dunne misjudging a long lob which bounced into our net. So the trip to Budapest was always going to be difficult with just a one-goal advantage.

'The journey was awful to say the least, delayed in London by a strike and with another hold-up in Brussels, but we were ready to give it a good go.

'Ferencvaros had a good player, Florian Albert, and he

Manchester United's success in the Sixties saw their star forwards in the headlines, but the team was built on a solid defence and the partnership of Nobby Stiles and centre half Bill Foulkes, up highest here against Sheffield Wednesday.

had a real tussle with Bill Foulkes. Just before the interval he got the ball to Varga who let fly with a shot. I flung myself to block it and stopped it with my shoulder.

'The referee gave a penalty against me for hand-ball. I thought it was a harsh decision. Novak scored with the spot-kick, and though we tried hard in the second half we lost 1-0 to finish on aggregate 3-3.

'They didn't have the system of away goals counting double in those days so it was a play-off — and we lost the toss.

'We had to go back to Budapest with me feeling terrible as the player responsible for the penalty which had forced the third game. The journey by road from Vienna to Budapest seemed never ending and by then it was June 16 when most footballers were on holiday.

'But we played well. In fact we paralysed them only to lose 2-1 because we couldn't put the ball into the net.

'So success in Europe eluded us for yet another season, though I still look back proudly on that period. We had won the championship at least and we certainly had a good team normally bursting with goals.

'We had five players in double figures with League goals. Denis Law scored 28 in the League, and had a grand total in all competitions of 39.

'David Herd scored 28 in League and Cup while John Connelly had a tally of 20, Bobby Charlton had 18 and George Best in his first full season had bagged 14.

'It was an attack dripping with scoring power and I shall always remember that season for some great football. It was a very good team and great to be a part of it.

'People said we used to play off the cuff without any tactics or planning, but in reality we were well organised and we had good players, which at the end of the day is what it is all about.'

Nobby played first-team football at Old Trafford for 11 seasons, making a total of 311 League appearances. He played in 37 European ties, including the Estudiantes match. He made 38 F.A. Cup appearances.

Nobby Stiles played nearly 400 League and Cup games for Old Trafford before cartilage trouble and a transfer to Middlesbrough.

Then at the age of 27 he suffered the effects of two cartilage operations during a period of change at the club.

David Sadler had taken his place and soon after the departure of Wilf McGuinness as manager in May, 1971, United accepted an offer of £20,000 for him from Middlesbrough.

After two seasons at Ayresome Park he moved for the same fee to play for Bobby Charlton at Preston. Altogether he was at Deepdale for eight years, quitting as a player after a year to spend three seasons as coach and then four as manager.

Early on in his career he had married Kay, the sister of his United chum John Giles, and after finishing at Preston he joined his brother-in-law in Canada. John was the manager of Vancouver Whitecaps and Nobby became his coach.

Later he followed Giles to West Bromwich Albion to do a similar job at the Hawthorns. He became youth team coach with the Albion, a role in football which he tells me he likes best, and then last summer, much to his delight, Manchester United brought him back to Old Trafford to work with Brian Kidd on the junior coaching staff.

One of his three sons, John, plays for Leeds United. The family still live in Sale, not far from Old Trafford.

Nobby walks around these days looking even less like a professional sportsman with his thick, black-rimmed glasses, but I remember him when he struck fear into opponents.

How could I forget the greeting the South Americans gave him when he walked throught the Buenos Aires Airport on his way to play Estudiantes?

A welcoming commentator boomed over the public address system: 'Bobby Charlton . . . El Supremo, George Best . . . El Beatle,' and then his voice went up an octave and a great roar went up as he shouted 'Nobby Stiles . . . El Bandido.'

NOBBY STILES' RECORD

	LEAGUE		F.A. CUP		F.L. CUP		EUROPE		TOTAL	
	App	Gls	App	Gls	App	Gls	App	Gls	App	Gls
1960-61	26	2	3		2				31	2
1961-62	34	7	4						38	7
1962-63	31	2	4						35	2
1963-64	17		2				2		25	
1964-65	41		7				11	1	49	1
1965-66	39	2	7				8	1	46	3
1966-67	37	3	2		1				40	3
1967-68	20						7		20	
1968-69	41	1	6				9	1	47	2
1969-70	8		3		2				13	
1970-71	17				2				19	
	311	17	38		7		37	3	393	20

NORTHERN IRELAND: 1965 v Scotland, Hungary, Yugoslavia, Sweden, Wales, Austria, Northern Ireland, Spain; 1966 v Poland, West Germany, Scotland, Norway, Denmark, Poland, Uruguay, Mexico, France, Argentina, Portugal, West Germany, Northern Ireland, Czechoslovakia, Wales; 1967 v Scotland; 1968 v USSR; 1969 v Rumania; 1970 v Northern Ireland, Scotland (28 caps).

CHAPTER TEN

Bryan Robson

Bryan Robson, skipper of Manchester United and England, is the Captain Fantastic of modern football.

He is the complete all-rounder, the player who can do virtually everything, and what's more, do it better than most. The unassuming Geordie is a man to build a team round, which of course is why Ron Atkinson set a record fee when he paid West Bromich Albion £1.5m to bring him to Old Trafford.

The beauty of Bryan is that time showed that he was a bargain buy.

Atkinson could be said to be biased after spending so much money on a midfield player, but Bobby Robson, the manager of England, is just as big an admirer.

With good cause, of course, because it could well be that Bryan Robson kept him in his job with his performances and vital goals when the England boss was under pressure following the disastrous campaign in the European championships in Germany in 1988.

England might well have fallen completely apart when the manager was being pilloried as a 'plonker' and tabloid newspaper headlines were screaming for him to go, but for the captain's steadying influence and efforts to secure some respectable results.

Bryan Robson was without doubt England's best player in Germany and one of the few to come home with his reputation intact. The team's failure must have hit him harder than most because time is running out for soccer's 'action man', and for a player of his stature he has few medals to show for his career.

He would dearly like to win something with England,

Bryan Robson has been one of the most influential players ever to wear a red shirt.

and a League championship with Manchester United remains a cherished dream; yet by the end of the 1989-90 season he will have turned 33.

Bryan has made no secret of the fact that the motivation behind leaving West Bromwich was to be with a club which won things, and he also turned down the chance of making his fortune in Italy in order to pursue his domestic ambitions with United.

Perhaps it is the absence of an elusive championship medal which keeps him going at Old Trafford. Certainly his drive and determination is as fierce as ever, and therefore considerable, because it has always been his presence as well as his personal ability which has marked him out as special.

For Robson is an influential, and an inspiring, player who brings out the best from those around him. He leads more by example than by orders so that when he does speak on the field of play it is with considerable effect.

Off the field he talks carefully and sensibly about football, and long experience has not dulled his appetite for the game. Alex Feguson, the manager of Manchester United, continues to see Robson as one of the players he can regard as a stable and known quantity.

This of course is how Ron Atkinson saw the player when he examined his resources on succeeding Dave Sexton as manager at Old Trafford in the summer of 1981.

He told me at the time that he considered there were good players in both defence and attack, but that he just couldn't see how United were going to stop the opposition tearing through the midfield.

The result was a return to his old club at The Hawthorns to work out a package valued at £2m for Remi Moses and Robson. With those two players in his side he achieved a high level of consistency twice winning the F.A. Cup and finishing in the top four in the League in all five seasons he was in the Old Trafford hot seat.

Ron Atkinson has remained a Robson enthusiast and agrees that for some time now the player has been the main prop for both his club and his country.

Manchester United broke the transfer record when they paid West Bromwich Albion £1.5m for Bryan Robson. So it was hardly surprising that they made the signing into a public ceremony out on the Old Trafford pitch. Left to right: Ron Atkinson (manager), Bryan Robson, Les Olive (secretary) and Martin Edwards (chairman).

He says: 'If Manchester United achieve success and England qualify for the World Cup in Italy in 1990 the bottom line won't be too hard to read . . . they will both have been carried there by Bryan Robson.

'Robbo has built himself into a colossus when so many

other players are seriously thinking of chucking their boots into the corner cupboard for good.

'He's 32 and still untouchable. It's no wonder they call him Captain Marvel. It was a disgrace when both the players and the football writers overlooked him when they were voting for their Players of the Year.

'Mark Hughes and Steve Nicol both had smashing seasons, but it was a crying shame when Robbo didn't get either of the awards. Too many injustices have stopped him over the years and it's terrible that he has never been actually honoured as Footballer of the Year.

'He's light years ahead of other players with what he has achieved for United. He has been the driving force, the player with his hand on the helm.

'It's the same story with England, and I believe both United and England should get down on their knees and pray that he carries on for a few more years yet, which he's certainly capable of doing if that's what he wants.

'I know that when I was manager of Atletico Madrid I was ready to offer Manchester United their money back and give £1.5m to take him to Spain.

'I had already got the blessing of Atletico President Jesus Gil because he knew like me that on the Continent Bryan could play until he's 40. He could be another Platini because in Europe there is less pressure, more room and not as many high-profile games so that somebody with "Pop's" appetite for football could go on for years.

'It would be like playing in an armchair for him.

'If I hadn't been given the sack in Madrid my next move was to have been an approach to Alex Ferguson to see if he could have been persuaded to do a deal.

'I have always considered that the two best half-backs in the history of the game have been Duncan Edwards and Dave Mackay. In my book Bryan Robson now stands shoulder to shoulder with the pair of them.

'I just hope he can win a championship medal before his time runs out. I believe he can, because he can always switch from midfield to play alongside the centre half to extend his career. He certainly deserves a League medal.'

Commitment is the name of the game for the captain of Manchester United as he shows in this derby action with Manchester City goalkeeper Joe Corrigan.

Robson's strength is his ability to bring together the art of the well-timed tackle and the vision to make good use of the ball once he has won it. His passing is invariably accurate, and it isn't always safe passing. He will put the ball into space and he will prompt movement in his own team in order to create an opening.

To that basic efficiency he adds a tremendous capacity for work, covering tirelessly yet always ready to make those driving runs into the opposition penalty box.

It's made him a midfield player who scores goals, an attribute for which Bobby Robson in particular will be eternally grateful.

As the England manager explained to me: 'After the European championships of 1986 everyone connected with the international scene took a lot of criticism.

'When the flak flies a lot of people keep their heads down, but you can't do that in football, at least not if you want to come through to more successful times.

'It's a situation which calls for players to stand up and be counted, and our captain did exactly that. He kept his head up and battled through to what I hope will be a more successful period for the England team.

'And if we do enjoy a little success, then a lot of it will be due to Bryan Robson who played when it really mattered, and by his example encouraged others to follow, and match his high standard.'

Robson's commitment was never better illustrated than when he played for Manchester United against Barcelona in the quarter-final of the European Cup Winners Cup of season 1983-84.

The captain felt he had let the team down in the first leg in Spain when he had missed chances and the Reds had come home with a 2-0 defeat.

The fans who felt that the second leg at Old Trafford against Maradona's team would be a formality for the Spanish club hadn't reckoned with Bryan Robson's reaction.

The Reds' skipper seemed to have made the return match a personal crusade. He was a man inspired as he scored twice to lead United to a memorable 3-0 victory and give the club their first European semi-final for 15 years on a marvellous night reminiscent of past glories.

The home fans burst on to the pitch at the end to carry the captain off on their shoulders. He deserved no less after a remarkable recovery which prompted the old master, Sir Matt Busby, to say: 'The memories came flooding back. The game took me right back to the time

Bryan took over the captaincy from another natural leader in Ray Wilkins and has been so outstanding that at one stage United were described as a one-man team.

we pulled back two goals against Bilbao at Maine Road for that memorable win in our first season in Europe in 1957.'

Robson recalls: 'I felt I was to blame for coming home two goals down from the first leg in the Nou Camp Stadium.

'Big games are all about putting the ball into the back of the net and a player of my experience should have done just that.

'I had two glorious chances and missed them both.

'The first was very early on. I tried to chip over the goalkeeper in a situation which should have seen me give him no chance.

'As it was he tipped the ball over the bar. Then later in the game I should have put a shot away instead of trying to reach Mark Hughes with a pass.

'If we're talking about standards, then I let myself and everyone else down. I was more to blame for the defeat than Graeme Hogg who was just unfortunate with his own-goal.

'At least we carved out some chances which was on the credit side and gave us hope for the second leg. It showed that Barcelona were at least vulnerable and that under pressure they might crack.'

And crack they did as the Reds came off the ropes led by a captain possessed. Robson scored in the 23rd minute with a bullet header after Norman Whiteside had flicked on a Ray Wilkins corner.

Five minutes after the interval he was hunting in the Barcelona goalmouth again to score his 17th goal of the season, pouncing on a loose ball after Urruti had failed to hold cleanly a shot from Wilkins.

Frank Stapleton drove in the third goal, but the night belonged to Robson, though with typical modesty he contented himself with a simple statement: 'After missing the chances in Barcelona I said that I owed the lads something, and I was just delighted I did it for them at Old Trafford.'

Robson's peformance against the likes of Diego Maradona and Berndt Schuster on the European stage inevitably made him an even more attractive target for foreign clubs with the Italians particularly interested.

United slapped what they considered to be a prohibitive transfer fee of £3m on him but speculation about a move abroad was still rife during the summer.

Much to the satisfaction of the supporters, all was resolved in the October of the following season when club and player agreed a new seven-year contract.

Robson was inspired when he led Manchester United to victory over Barcelona at Old Trafford in the European Cup Winners Cup in 1984. United trailed 2-0 from the first leg in Spain and an inspired skipper scored twice in the second leg for a 3-0 win on a memorable night. The player was hoisted shoulder high by jubilant fans on the pitch.

Chairman Martin Edwards said at the time: 'The length and worth of the contract is a record in Britain. At the same time there is an element of personal financial sacrifice by the player who could have kept himself available for a move to Italy at a later stage.

'We never really wanted to sell him during the summer and we thought the £3m price tag would frighten people off. We came in for quite a lot of hammer but we hope this contract makes it clear that we want to keep our captain and most influential player.

'Bryan has made it just as clear that money is not everything to him either. It's a good contract but modest compared with Italian money. I cannot commend his attitude enough and we are delighted to have him for the next seven years.'

Naturally enough the player has seized other opportunities to look after his financial future. He has enjoyed several lucrative endorsements linking him with jeans and sports shoes including his own brand of football boot. He is a partner in a thriving greetings card business which has outlets over a wide part of the country.

Bryan and his wife Denise, a Birmingham girl he met in his days as a West Bromwich player, live with their three children in Hale, Cheshire, but considering his position as England's top football man, without ostentation.

You get the impression that Bryan Robson will not be forgetting his roots in Chester-le-Street, County Durham, where his father was a long-distance lorry driver and he grew up with a sister, and two younger brothers who both followed him into professional football, though perhaps with not quite the same success.

Like so many of the greats in this book, Bryan started out as an unlikely-looking footballer. He had skill and energy, but like George Best, Denis Law and Nobby Stiles before him, he was another shrimp!

He was spotted playing in a schoolboy match by Bill Emery, the scout who represented West Bromwich Albion in the North East. Emery went round to the youngster's home and noted: 'Bryan was a small lad but he had a very alert look about him. He was very quiet, not shy, just quiet.'

Bryan was sent down to the Midlands for trials and became a schoolboy signing. He went for training during the holidays and to play in the occasional match. He still didn't grow very much, though, and when he reached 15 and a decision had to be taken on whether to make him an apprentice on the club staff his future was very much in the balance.

Don Howe, later the England coach, was Albion's manager and he admits now: 'In those days we were allowed a maximum of 15 apprentices so I asked our chief scout Reg Ryan how many we had agreed to take that year. He said 11, so I said well we've got some space. We'll tell his father we'll give the boy a chance but we have reservations and are not a hundred per cent.'

Later Don said: 'He was small but you can sense when a young man has something. Looking at him I thought he had got character, an inner confidence.'

It was a very perceptive assessment, though it was still some time before it was apparent for all to see.

Bryan Robson has also known the dark side during his career. He lies in agony here on the running track with a dislocated shoulder after crashing into the advertising boards, an injury which was to wreck England's World Cup campaign in the 1986 World Cup in Mexico.

After a month as an apprentice, Bryan phoned the scout who had encouraged him and who had sent him to The Hawthorns to say he wasn't happy. It wasn't homesickness but simply that he wasn't showing up too well against the other youngsters.

'I'm last in all the sprints and shuttles,' he said.

Emery spoke to the club and was reassured that though the youngster was frequently last, there was no need to worry because he thought quicker than most of the others.

Howe confirmed: 'Often enough Bryan would be in a shirt that was too big for him, beating the larger boys, and he started to look a good 'un. The coaches told me he had this tremendous energy level.'

Albion worked on him in training and back at his digs his landlady started every day for him with a cocktail of raw egg, milk, sherry and sugar followed every evening with a nightcap of a bottle of Mackeson.

Size and strength were not his only obstacles. In season 1976-77 he broke his leg not once, but three times.

The first time was playing against Spurs when he was kicked as he made a tackle. He came back too quickly after just eight weeks and fractured his leg in the same place playing for the reserves. He recovered but just before the end of the same season he broke his other leg playing against Manchester City and was out of action for four months.

Says Brian: 'I lost a year. The worst part was that it happened before I was established. When you are recognised and are injured everyone is waiting for your return, but when you have never been there, you just get forgotten.'

Bryan had made his first-team debut under Johnny Giles who said: 'In two years Bryan became a man very quickly. He got physically stronger and his confidence grew.'

The arrival of Ron Atkinson as Albion manager in 1978 saw him confirmed as a player of immense potential. He became a key man at West Bromwich and was picked for the England Under-21 team, making his full England debut against Hungary in 1981.

He had a good rapport with Ron Atkinson and when his manager moved to Manchester United in the summer of 1981 he needed little persuasion to follow him.

Ronnie Allen, who had succeeded Atkinson, fought hard to keep the player and stuck a powerful £2m fee on him to try to deter United, but as Bryan explained: 'I had been with Albion for eight years and felt I needed a change.

'They didn't seem to be thinking of themselves as a big club. When top players came up for sale you never heard of West Brom making offers. I wanted a big club with big ideas at that point in my career.

'I wanted to win things which is why I was happy to join Manchester United.'

Bryan signed on for the Reds out on the pitch before the

No-one tried harder for a beleaguered Bobby Robson than his England captain after the disappointment of an early exit from the European championships in Germany in 1988.

kick-off against Wolves on October 3, 1981. Ironically his new team went on to win 5-0 with a hat-trick from Sammy McIlroy.

His League debut came in the following game against

Manchester City at Maine Road in front of a 52,037 crowd. He played solidly in a goalless derby.

He had no cause to regret his transfer, with the Reds finishing in an encouraging third place in his first season. The following season fully justified his move, with United reaching two cup finals at Wembley.

Robson missed the Milk Cup final against Liverpool with torn ankle ligaments and the Anfield club won 2-1 in extra time. It wasn't United's day. They lost Kevin Moran with injury and finished with Gordon McQueen hobbling on the wing while Lou Macari played at full back.

Even so it was a closely run match, and if Robson had played he might just have made the difference.

United fought their way back to Wembley to meet Brighton in the final of the F.A. Cup and this time Robson was in the thick of the action all the way. The Reds made a hash of their first game which ended 2-2 after extra-time, but won the replay emphatically 4-0.

Robson was in one of his uncompromising moods again. He scored the first vital goal himself, and after Norman Whiteside had put United further ahead, Bryan made sure of victory with a goal from Frank Stapleton's header just before the interval.

The fourth goal, a penalty by Arnold Muhren, was a result of a foul on Robson as the team dynamo drove United to the kind of glory which had prompted his departure from West Bromwich.

The following season saw United finish fourth, with a personal contribution of 12 goals from 33 appearances . . . if only the Reds had been able to find a couple of strikers to match Robson's effort from midfield they might well have taken their title challenge a little closer.

This was the season which saw Bryan pull out his superlative effort against Barcelona in the European Cup Winners Cup before United lost a semi-final against Juventus, significantly without an injured Robson!

But the following year, 1984-85, saw another glorious return to Wembley after a cracking semi-final win over Liverpool with the help of a replay at Maine Road.

In the final Robson's men finished playing Everton with only 10 men following the dismissal of Kevin Moran, but they raised their game for Norman Whiteside to score in a 1-0 victory in extra time.

Season 1985-86 saw United make the kind of start which Robon believed would bring his dream of a championship medal into reality. The Reds won their first 10 League games, a glorious opening and a club record.

But then things went wrong for both the team and their captain. Robson tore his hamstring playing for England and aggravated the injury in a comeback game at Sheffield Wednesday. When he finally got back he twisted his ankle. His frustration saw him sent off for the first time in his career in a Cup tie at Sunderland.

But there was worse to come when Bryan fell heavily at West Ham, dislocating again the shoulder he had first damaged the previous season when he had crashed into advertising hoardings at Old Trafford against Coventry.

With the 1986 World Cup in Mexico looming, England manager Bobby Robson wanted the player to have an operation, but Ron Atkinson and Bryan refused; they thought there was still a chance of winning the championship.

As it turned out, United finished fourth and Bryan had been able to make only 21 League appearances in what had been a nightmare season with the succession of injuries making it look as if Action Man was coming apart at the seams.

Bryan went to the World Cup but playing against Mexico in a warm-up match he dislocated the shoulder for a third time. The England boss knew it was unlikely that he would be able to start the tournament with his captain in the line-up — especially when he also pulled his troublesome hamstring in a training game!

But his captain surprised him and declared himself fit to play with the help of a special harness to keep his shoulder in place. Bryan played for 75 minutes of a 1-0 defeat and played in the next game, a draw against Morocco, until he was bowled over and dislocated the shoulder yet again.

Although he said he was ready to play against Poland, the manager wouldn't risk it again, and it was the end of the player's sad saga in Mexico.

Eventually he flew home to have the shoulder pinned to leave the manager declaring at the end of the competition: 'With a fully fit Bryan Robson we would have won the World Cup.'

Robson missed the start of the next season, but once back he picked up his game with characteristic courage. Alex Ferguson arrived to take over from the sacked Ron Atkinson in November, and the new manager was soon enthusing about his skipper.

A great many people considered Robson's career as good as finished in 1986, but despite passing the 30-year-old mark he has played as well as ever.

Season 1987-88, for instance, when United finished second in the League to Liverpool, Bryan Robson made 36 League appearances and scored 11 goals.

His international form, despite playing in an unsuccessful team in the European championships in 1988, was top-class and at the time of writing he is the inspiration behind qualifying for the World Cup in Italy in 1990.

Season 1988-89 at Old Trafford was a troubled campaign with the team sliding into 11th place, and certainly 'Robbo', celebrating his 33rd birthday in January, 1990, could do with a little more support in midfield if he is to achieve his championship dream before he runs out of time.

One thing for sure, though, is that Captain Courageous will play to his last gasp until the moment he decides to hang up his boots.

BRYAN ROBSON'S RECORD

	LEAGUE		F.A. CUP		MILK/ LITTLEWOODS CUP		EUROPE		TOTAL	
	App	Gls	App	Gls	App	Gls	App	Gls	App	Gls
1981-82	32	5	1		2				35	5
1982-83	33	10	6	3	8	1	2	1	49	15
1983-84	33	12	1		6		6	4	46	16
1984-85	32/1	9	4	2	2	1	7	2	45/1	14
1985-86	21	7	3		2				26	7
1986-87	29	7			3				32	7
1987-88	36	11	2		5				43	11
1988-89	34	4	6	2	3	2			43	8
	250/1	65	23	7	31	4	15	7	319/1	83

ENGLAND: 1980 v Republic of Ireland, Australia, Norway, Rumania, Switzerland; 1981 v Spain, Rumania, Brazil, Wales, Scotland, Switzerland, Hungary (2), Norway; 1982 v Northern Ireland, Wales, Holland, Scotland, Finland, France, Czechoslovakia, West Germany, Spain, Denmark, Greece, Luxembourg; 1983 v Scotland, Hungary, Luxembourg; 1984 v France, Northern Ireland, Scotland, USSR, Brazil, Uruguay, Chile, East Germany, Finland, Turkey; 1985 v Republic of Ireland, Rumania, Finland, Scotland, Italy, Mexico, West Germany, USA, Rumania, Turkey; 1986 v Israel, Mexico, Portugal, Morocco, Northern Ireland; 1987 v Northern Ireland, Spain, Turkey, Brazil, Scotland; 1988 v Turkey, Yugoslavia, Holland (2), Hungary, Scotland, Columbia, Switzerland, Republic of Ireland, USSR; 1989 v Albania (2), Sweden, Poland, Denmark (2), Saudi Arabia, Greece, Chile, Scotland (78 caps).

CHAPTER ELEVEN

Mark Hughes

They call him thunder thighs . . . and anyone who has seen Mark Hughes in action will understand why.

His legs are like tree trunks, and now that he has added skill to his strength, the Manchester United striker is possibly the most fearsome forward in Britain.

His fellow professionals certainly thought so after trying to cope with his marauding menace in his first season back in English football following his sojourn in Spain and Germany.

The Professional Footballers Association unhesitatingly voted him their Player of the Year for 1989 ahead of such luminaries as his United skipper Bryan Robson and Liverpool's Steve Nicol who went on to win the Football Writers award.

There is little doubt that Mark came back a much improved player after playing for Barcelona and Bayern Munich.

Everton captain Kevin Ratcliffe who knows Hughes as well as any player after playing against him at club level and then behind him for Wales explains the difference: 'Mark has earned more respect from opponents since he has been back in English football.

'He didn't always use his aggression the right way before he left United, and that didn't make him too popular with his fellow professionals. Of course he was only 21 then and he is a lot more experienced now.

'Playing in Spain and Germany taught him to channel his strength and power. That's why defenders now don't relish playing against him.

'When United played at Goodison in his first season back

Mark Hughes joined Manchester United as a schoolboy and burst on to the first-team scene with some spectacular scoring.

we were lucky to get a draw. Mark's movement that day was brilliant and you could sense he had a point to prove.

'He's never been a prolific scorer but he is concentrating on getting into the box more.'

The choice of Hughes as Footballer of the Year followed his success of four years earlier when he was the PFA

Young Player of the Year, a double which immediately attracted the attention of Scottish international Andy Gray who won both awards in the same season.

Gray said: 'I can't think of anyone who deserved the honour more. It's very rare that a player is a success second time around, but Mark seems to get better every time I see him.

'He's not the biggest of lads but he's got such powerful thigh muscles he is able to shield the ball and lead the line so well. When United's defenders want a breather they've only to find him and they know the ball's not going to come straight back.

'He gives defenders the hardest 90 minutes in the First Division, and he was certainly my Player of the Year.'

It's difficult to know whether it was the departure of Mark Hughes or his return two years later which caused the bigger stir among United fans.

Certainly the decision to sell him to Barcelona for £1.8m was a shock to Old Trafford supporters who are not used to seeing their young stars lured away. Indeed many of them were angry and saw the sale as a betrayal.

In fact there were very good business reasons for selling Hughes when they did. The fact was that Hughes was due to complete his United contract in the summer of 1986. United had offered him a new agreement to stay on at Old Trafford, but he was advised by his agent to refuse it so that at the end of the season he would be a free agent and in a position to respond to the overtures which were being made from abroad.

It made sense from the player's point of view, but faced United with the prospect of receiving a European computed fee of around £350,000 for a striker being valued on the open market at £2m.

United basically didn't want to sell Hughes, but manager Ron Atkinson and chairman Martin Edwards knew that the player was intent on cashing in on the fortune that lay waiting for him abroad.

The only thing they could do in the circumstances was

The player soon started to win awards and here he collects his keys as the Fiat Young Player of the Year.

to make the best out of a bad job and at least ensure that they got as much money as possible for the player.

So they jumped at the idea put to them by an agent which was to give the player a new contract which included a clause stipulating that anyone wishing to buy him must pay £2m, in return for which the player had the freedom to move at the end of each season.

As Atkinson explained at the time: 'Mark wouldn't sign a normal contract, so we did the next best thing and entered into a contract which meant we had financial protection for our valuable asset.

'It hurt to concede that there are clubs in Europe with more financial clout than Manchester United, but it is a fact of life I'm afraid.'

The new agreement was signed midway through the 1985-86 season, and had the immediate advantage of keeping what United hoped would be a happy Hughes as they made their bid to win the championship after making their record start to the season of 10 successive wins.

United in fact went 15 matches before their first League defeat, a period conspicuous for goals by the 22-year-old Welshman. He scored 10 goals in that unbeaten run as the Reds raced into a commanding lead at the top of the table.

What no-one bargained for was the way Hughes went off the boil once the new deal had been signed. Barcelona insisted on the whole agreement being kept secret, so from the fans point of view, the player's loss of form was a complete mystery.

When a national newspaper revealed details of the deal in the March the anger of the supporters boiled over and they were hardly in the mood to listen to the financial arguments; most people only saw United involved in a money-making machination which had put a very good chance of winning the championship at risk.

The controversy did nothing to help Hughes recover his form and with Bryan Robson running into injury problems as well the team went to pieces.

By mid-March Everton who at one point had been 17 points behind United were six points in front. Atkinson even dropped Hughes in a desperate attempt to get back on course.

Hughes scored three goals in the last four games, but it was too late to retrieve the situation as Liverpool came galloping through to take the title with Manchester United trailing in at fourth, 12 points behind the winners.

It was a bitter disappointment after such a brilliant opening to the season and the Hughes affair focused criticism of the chairman and sharpened the knives for Ron Atkinson who was sacked halfway through the following season.

United had held a 10-point lead in the October, yet by the end of the season leaflets were being distributed calling for Atkinson to be sacked.

It was tough because just as he couldn't be held responsible for Robson's injury problems, the Hughes contract was undoubtedly imposed on him from above.

Barcelona raided English football for two of the best marksmen and teamed Mark up with Gary Lineker. Here they are proudly paraded by another Englishman, Alan Harris, the Spanish Club coach.

Certainly the situation had been badly handled. The secrecy was a big mistake because when the news broke it came not from United themselves but as a revelation in a newspaper which immediately put the club at a disadvantage and made them look as if they had been caught with their hand in the till.

Even Hughes regretted the cloud of mystery which hung over his last months at Old Trafford. Surprisingly enough the fans blamed the club rather than the player and didn't seem to hold the transfer against Hughes himself.

Hughes in fact departed for his eight-year contract at Barcelona with fond memories of both club and supporters, as he explained to me: 'My fear was that the fans would turn against me when they found out I was going to Spain, but they didn't and I thank them for that. I had a lot of letters but not one nasty one.

'With hindsight it might have been better if the news had come out into the open in the January when the agreement was made. Instead I had to deny everything when the rumours started and I don't think it helped my form.

'One thing I would stress is that the club wanted me to stay. They made me a very good offer, but it couldn't really compare with the opportunity Barcelona offered me.

'It was a chance and a challenge I had to take, though I felt very emotional when the fans gave me their farewell at Old Trafford on my last home game.

'I had spent all my football life at Old Trafford from being a boy and when I went I left a part of me with United.'

The fans clearly didn't blame the player personally for his ambition and decision to seek fame and fortune in Spain. Perhaps they appreciated that apart from the final frustrating weeks he had always given a hundred per cent in the junior and reserve teams as well as supplying a lot of exciting football along with some memorable goals.

Mark also managed to keep one foot in the Old Trafford door when he said: 'When I come back to England there would be only one club I would want to join. Manchester United would be the team because they are the only club in Britain as far as I am concerned.'

It turned out that he wasn't just making a diplomatic departure. First, though, he had two years' exile abroad and the first year with Terry Venables at Barcelona was not at all what he had hoped for.

He found Spanish football difficult, so much so that in his second season he was packed off on loan to Germany to play for Bayern Munich where he was much happier.

Why did it all turn sour?

'When I left United, my style was a bit over-physical. If someone kicked me, I took it personally and tried to kick them back. My aggression in Spain got me into trouble, even when I didn't actually do anything wrong,' he explained.

'I had to curb my style and once some of the aggression went out of my game I was only half the player I had been in England.

'It was never going to be easy. I had only been in United's

Mark Hughes received the highest possible accolade from his fellow professionals when they voted him the Players' Player of the Year in 1989. With him is Arsenal's Paul Merson, the PFA Young Player of the Year.

first team for a couple of seasons before I went to Spain and the demands are so high at Barcelona. The Spanish crowds don't have much patience. They want success instantly and they don't give much help if things are going badly.

'The foreign player is an easy target. People are often just waiting for you to fail.

'It didn't help that the build-up was so slow. I never seemed to have the chance to catch defenders on the hop. Gary Lineker did better because of his pace.

'I wasn't scoring goals so I gave the critics plenty of ammunition. Eventually it came as a relief to be left out of the side.

'At the time of my move I wasn't married to Jill and although she used to fly out now and again I didn't have a settled home life.

'I was glad to go on loan to Bayern. I enjoyed myself there. German football suited me better and I will always be grateful to Uli Hoeness for getting my career off the ground again.

'They actually wanted to sign me and if United hadn't been interested I would have done.

'I'll never regret going abroad, even though it didn't work out as I planned. The whole experience of living and working on the Continent broadened me and I think I came back a more mature person.

'I also think I am a more complete player. The different styles in Europe taught me more options, and I think I have learned to use my aggression properly.'

Manager Alex Ferguson made Hughes one of his first transfer targets. He tried unsuccessfully to bring him home just before Barcelona farmed him out to Bayern Munich, but at that stage Venables wanted to keep the striker in reserve.

In the summer of 1987 he finally clinched a deal for a player he feels should never have been allowed to leave Old Trafford.

'I felt it was a mistake for the club to have sold him in the first place, but he wanted to go abroad and perhaps now he has got it out of his system. I certainly think he was happy to return to United and I was delighted to have him.

'I have never seen a player with so much strength. He's really an awesome sight at close quarters,' says the United manager.

Hughes joined United second time around on a five-year contract saying: 'Of course money is important, but so is making a success of your career, and I believe the next few years are going to be successful both for myself and Manchester United.'

Manchester United fans were delighted when manager Alex Ferguson moved determinedly to bring Mark back to Old Trafford in a club record £1.8m transfer.

Mark was born at Wrexham and was bright at school as well as always looking a promising footballer.

He finished with six O levels but as his mother, Jenny, says: 'I thought he might go on to be academic, but once a scout from Manchester United knocked on the door I realised there was only going to be one career for him.'

He certainly had other talents as a youngster and he played the violin in the school orchestra until he decided that carrying a violin case on the bus to school made him look a cissy.

His primary school teacher has a casette of a lovely treble voice singing 'O Little Town of Bethlehem' at a Christmas carol service in a Ruabon Church.

It seems a far cry from the tough guy striker he has become, though as his old teacher says: 'He was the nicest lad you could wish to meet until you put him on a football field. Then it was a Jekyll and Hyde job.

'He was everywhere, knocking all the others out of the way to get the ball, taking the goalkicks, the free-kicks, the corner kicks and scoring all the goals.

'When we started a team at our primary school he was only eight and the smallest boy in the side but even then he was outstanding. He was an intelligent lad and I told him to stick to his studies but I always knew he would finish as a professional footballer.

'I'm proud that I had him as a pupil, but even prouder when I see him in the town now and realise he hasn't changed. He is still a lovely lad.'

Still a modest, unassuming man who tends to run a mile from publicity, he has always kept in close touch with his roots in Wrexham and lifelong pals in the Duke of Wellington at Ruabon.

Born in November, 1963, he joined United as an apprentice at the age of 16. Wales capped him at all levels from schoolboy to full senior, and it was undoubtedly some of the spectacular goals he scored on the international stage which first attracted attention from abroad.

His first major contribution for United was in the F.A. Youth Cup of season 1981-82 when he teamed up with Norman Whiteside to give the Reds a powerful strike force for junior level.

The youngsters reached the final with the likes of Clayton Blackmore, Billy Garton, Graeme Hogg and Mark Dempsey in the side with them.

They lost the first leg at Old Trafford 3-2 against Watford, and then staged a remarkable recovery at Vicarage Road to draw 4-4 with Mark supplying two of the goals.

It wasn't enough to win on aggregate of course, but reaching the final for the first time in 18 years was an encouraging step down the right road and an indication of a promising crop of starlets.

Although 18 months older than Whiteside, Mark didn't progress quite as quickly as the Irishman, and his full League debut didn't come until March, 1984, when he played against Leicester City at Old Trafford and scored in a 2-0 win.

He made seven full appearances that season plus coming on in four games as a substitute . . . and scored four goals, a highly encouraging start.

On tour in pre-season games tuning up for the next campaign he emerged as the leading scorer and was rewarded with a place in the starting line-up at the expense of Whiteside. The only problem that year was finding the right partner from Alan Brazil, Whiteside and Frank Stapleton who were all paired with him at different times.

Hughes retained the number one striker role, though, and in all competitions he notched 25 goals, the best individual scoring performance at United for 13 years. In fact he only needed a couple more goals to have become the best since the glory days of George Best in the 1968 European Cup winning season.

A brilliant season blending goals with exciting work on the ball won him the Professional Footballer Association vote as Young Player of the Year.

A delighted Ron Atkinson said: 'He matured an awful lot. An injury to Frank Stapleton gave him a chance and he started to express himself more, free of Frank's shadow.

'He is still a shy, quiet boy, but once on the field he played with telling effect. He is strong and confident on the ball and I love to see the way he controls it. So do the fans. There is no limit to what he can achieve.'

His partnership for Wales with Liverpool's Ian Rush was hailed as one of the best in Europe. The goal he volleyed home against Scotland at Hampden Park will be long remembered. It was little wonder the foreign clubs homed in on Old Trafford the following season, especially after United's whirlwind winning opening.

By Christmas he was booked for Barcelona. Now he is back and playing even better, though we have yet to see the full potential of his United partnership with Brian McClair.

Hughes was United's leading League scorer with 14 goals in his first season back in English football and he finished with a total in all competitions of 16.

McClair scored 10 in the League in an overall tally of 17. Both strikers were scoring, but each had a dry run and manager Alex Ferguson is convinced they will both do better after working on the partnership.

Manchester United's chances of honours will depend to a large extent on whether the manager is right, and certainly he is entitled to be optimistic, particularly with a strengthened midfield.

It might well be early days to elevate Mark Hughes into the company of the other great footballers who grace this book; after all he has little to show in answer to that time honoured challenge: Show us your medals!

But the Welshman is included because he promises so much for the future and has packed more experience into his 25 years than most footballers see in a lifetime.

Mark Hughes is so well equipped to take us to the stars in our theatre of dreams at Old Trafford.

MARK HUGHES' RECORD

	LEAGUE		F.A. CUP		MILK/ LITTLEWOODS CUP		EUROPE		TOTAL	
	App	Gls	App	Gls	App	Gls	App	Gls	App	Gls
1983-84	7	4			1	1	2		10	5
1984-85	38	16	7	4	2	3	8	2	55	25
1985-86	40	17	3	1	2				45	18
1986-87	Barcelona									
1987-88	Barcelona/Bayern Munich									
1988-89	38	14	7	2	3				48	16
	123	51	17	7	8	4	10	2	158	64

WALES: 1984 v England, Northern Ireland; 1985 v Iceland (2), Spain (2), Norway (2), Scotland; 1986 v Scotland, Hungary, Uruguay; 1987 v Russia, Czechoslovakia (2), Denmark (2), 1988 v Sweden, Malta, Italy; 1989 v Finland, Holland, West Germany. (23 caps).

Manchester United Honours

European Cup
Winners: 1968
Semi-Finalists: 1957 1958 1966 1969

World Club Championship
Finalists: 1968

Football League Division One
Champions: 1908 1911 1952 1956 1957 1965 1967
Runners-up: 1947 1948 1949 1951 1959 1964 1968 1980

Football League Division Two
Champions: 1936 1975
Runners-up: 1897 1906 1925 1938

F.A. Challenge Cup
Winners: 1909 1948 1963 1977 1983 1985
Finalists: 1957 1958 1976 1979
Semi-Finalists: 1926 1949 1962 1964 1965 1966 1970

Football League Cup
Finalists: 1983
Semi-Finalists: 1970 1971 1975

European Cup Winners Cup
Semi-Finalists: 1984

Inter-Cities Fairs Cup
Semi-Finalists: 1965

F.A. Youth Cup
Winners: 1953 1954 1955 1956 1957 1964
Finalists: 1982 1986

Season	P	W	D	L	F	A	Pts	Position
				DIVISION I				
1946/47	42	22	12	8	95	54	56	2nd
1947/48	42	19	14	9	81	48	52	2nd
1948/49	42	21	11	10	77	44	53	2nd
1949/50	42	18	14	10	69	44	50	4th
1950/51	42	24	8	10	74	40	56	2nd
1951/52	42	23	11	8	95	52	57	CHAMPIONS
1952/53	42	18	10	14	69	72	46	8th
1953/54	42	18	12	12	73	58	48	4th
1954/55	42	20	7	15	84	74	47	5th
1955/56	42	25	10	7	83	51	60	CHAMPIONS
1956/57	42	28	8	6	103	54	64	CHAMPIONS
1957/58	42	16	11	15	85	75	43	9th
1958/59	42	24	7	11	103	66	55	2nd
1959/60	42	19	7	16	102	80	45	7th
1960/61	42	18	9	15	88	76	45	7th
1961/62	42	15	9	18	72	75	39	15th
1962/63	42	12	10	20	67	81	34	19th
1963/64	42	23	7	12	90	62	53	2nd
1964/65	42	26	9	7	89	39	61	CHAMPIONS
1965/66	42	18	15	9	84	59	51	4th
1966/67	42	24	12	6	84	45	60	CHAMPIONS
1967/68	42	24	8	10	89	55	56	2nd
1968/69	42	15	12	15	57	53	42	11th
1969/70	42	14	17	11	66	61	45	8th
1970/71	42	16	11	15	65	66	43	8th
1971/72	42	19	10	13	69	61	48	8th
1972/73	42	12	13	17	44	60	37	18th
1973/74	42	10	12	20	38	48	32	21st
				DIVISION II				
1974/75	42	26	9	7	66	30	61	1st
				DIVISION I				
1975/76	42	23	10	9	68	42	56	3rd
1976/77	42	18	11	13	71	62	47	6th
1977/78	42	16	10	16	67	63	42	10th
1978/79	42	15	15	12	60	63	45	9th
1979/80	42	24	10	8	65	35	58	2nd
1980/81	42	15	18	9	51	36	48	8th

1981/82	42	22	12	8	59	29	78	3rd
1982/83	42	19	13	10	56	38	70	3rd
1983/84	42	20	14	8	71	41	74	4th
1984/85	42	22	10	10	77	47	76	4th
1985/86	42	22	10	10	70	36	76	4th
1986/87	42	14	14	14	52	45	56	11th
1987/88	40	23	12	5	71	38	81	2nd
1988/89	38	13	12	13	45	35	51	11th

F.A. CUP RECORD

(United scores first)

1946-47

Round 3	Bradford	(a)	3-0
Round 4	Nottingham Forest	(h)	0-2

1947-48

Round 3	Aston Villa	(a)	6-4
Round 4	Liverpool	(Goodison)	3-0
Round 5	Charlton Athletic	(Leeds Rd)	2-0
Round 6	Preston North End	(Maine Rd)	4-1
Semi-Final	Derby County	(Hillsborough)	3-1
Final	Blackpool	(Wembley)	4-2

1948-49

Round 3	Bournemouth	(h)	6-0
Round 4	Bradford	(h)	1-1
	Bradford	(a)	1-1
	Bradford	(Maine Rd)	5-0
Round 5	Yeovil Town	(h)	8-0
Round 6	Hull City	(a)	1-0
Semi-Final	Wolves	(Hillsborough)	1-1
	Wolves	(Goodison)	0-1

1949-50

Round 3	Weymouth	(h)	4-0
Round 4	Watford	(a)	1-0
Round 5	Portsmouth	(h)	3-3
	Portsmouth	(a)	3-1
Round 6	Chelsea	(a)	0-2

1950-51

Round 3	Oldham Athletic	(h)	4-1
Round 4	Leeds United	(h)	4-1
Round 5	Arsenal	(h)	1-0
Round 6	Birmingham City	(a)	0-1

1951-52

Round 3	Hull City	(h)	0-2

1952-53

Round 3	Millwall	(a)	1-0
Round 4	Walthamstowe	(h)	1-1
	Walthamstowe	(a)	5-2
Round 5	Everton	(a)	1-2

1953-54

Round 3	Burnley	(a)	3-5

1954-55

Round 3	Reading	(a)	1-1
	Reading	(h)	4-1
Round 4	Manchester City	(a)	0-2

1955-56

Round 3	Bristol Rovers	(a)	0-4

1956-57

Round 3	Hartlepool	(a)	4-3
Round 4	Wrexham	(a)	5-0
Round 5	Everton	(h)	1-0
Round 6	Bournemouth	(a)	2-1
Semi-Final	Birmingham	(Hillsborough)	2-0
Final	Aston Villa	(Wembley)	1-2

1957-58

Round 3	Workington	(a)	3-1
Round 4	Ipswich Town	(h)	2-0
Round 5	Sheffield Wednesday	(h)	3-0
Round 6	West Brom	(a)	2-2
	West Brom	(h)	1-0
Semi-Final	Fulham	(Villa Park)	2-2
	Fulham	(Highbury)	5-3
Final	Bolton	(Wembley)	0-2

1958-59

Round 3	Norwich	(a)	0-3

1959-60

Round 3	Derby County	(a)	4-2
Round 4	Liverpool	(a)	3-1
Round 5	Sheffield Wednesday	(h)	0-1

1960-61

Round 3	Middlesbrough	(h)	3-0
Round 4	Sheffield Wednesday	(a)	1-1
	Sheffield Wednesday	(h)	2-7

1961-62

Round 3	Bolton	(h)	2-1
Round 4	Arsenal	(h)	1-0
Round 5	Sheffield Wednesday	(h)	0-0
	Sheffield Wednesday	(a)	2-0
Round 6	Preston	(a)	0-0
	Preston	(h)	2-1
Semi-Final	Spurs	(Hillsborough)	1-3

1962-63

Round 3	Huddersfield	(h)	5-0
Round 4	Aston Villa	(h)	1-0
Round 5	Chelsea	(h)	2-1
Round 6	Coventry	(a)	3-1
Semi-Final	Southampton	(Villa Park)	1-0
Final	Leicester City	(Wembley)	3-1

1963-64

Round 3	Southampton	(a)	3-2
Round 4	Bristol Rovers	(h)	4-1
Round 5	Barnsley	(a)	4-0
Round 6	Sunderland	(h)	3-3
	Sunderland	(a)	2-2
	Sunderland	(Leeds Rd)	5-1
Semi-Final	West Ham United	(Hillsborough)	1-3

1964-65

Round 3	Chester	(h)	2-1
Round 4	Stoke	(a)	0-0
	Stoke	(h)	1-0
Round 5	Barnsley	(h)	2-1
Round 6	Wolves	(a)	5-3
Semi-Final	Leeds United	(Hillsborough)	0-0
	Leeds United	(Nott. Forest)	0-1

1965-66

Round 3	Derby County	(a)	5-2
Round 4	Rotherham United	(h)	0-0
	Rotherham United	(a)	1-0
Round 5	Wolves	(a)	4-2
Round 6	Preston North End	(a)	1-1
	Preston North End	(h)	3-1
Semi-Final	Everton	(Burnden Park)	0-1

1966-67

Round 3	Stoke City	(h)	2-1
Round 4	Norwich	(h)	1-2

1967-68

Round 3	Spurs	(h)	2-2
	Spurs	(a)	0-1

1968-69

Round 3	Exeter City	(a)	3-1
Round 4	Watford	(h)	1-1
	Watford	(a)	2-0
Round 5	Birmingham	(a)	2-2
	Birmingham	(h)	6-2
Round 6	Everton	(h)	0-1

1969-70

Round 3	Ipswich Town	(a)	1-0
Round 4	Manchester City	(h)	3-0
Round 5	Northampton	(a)	8-2
Round 6	Middlesbrough	(a)	1-1
	Middlesbrough	(h)	2-1
Semi-Final	Leeds United	(Hillsborough)	0-0
	Leeds United	(Villa Park)	0-0
	Leeds United	(Burnden Park)	0-1

1970-71

Round 3	Middlesbrough	(h)	0-0
	Middlesbrough	(a)	1-2

1971-72

Round 3	Southampton	(a)	1-1
	Southampton	(h)	4-1
Round 4	Preston North End	(a)	2-0
Round 5	Middlesbrough	(h)	0-0
	Middlesbrough	(a)	3-0
Round 6	Stoke City	(h)	1-1
	Stoke City	(a)	1-2

1972-73

Round 3	Wolves	(a)	0-1

1973-74

Round 3	Plymouth Argyle	(h)	1-0
Round 4	Ipswich Town	(h)	0-1

1974-75

Round 3	Walsall	(h)	0-0
	Walsall	(a)	2-3

1975-76

Round 3	Oxford United	(h)	2-1
Round 4	Peterborough United	(h)	3-1
Round 5	Leicester City	(a)	2-1
Round 6	Wolves	(h)	1-1
	Wolves	(a)	3-2
Semi-Final	Derby County	(Hillsborough)	2-0
Final	Southampton	(Wembley)	0-1

1976-77

Round 3	Walsall	(h)	1-0
Round 4	Queens Park Rangers	(h)	1-0
Round 5	Southampton	(a)	2-2
	Southampton	(h)	2-1
Round 6	Aston Villa	(h)	2-1
Semi Final	Leeds United	(Villa Park)	2-1
Final	Liverpool	(Wembley)	2-1

1977-78

Round 3	Carlisle	(a)	1-1
	Carlisle	(h)	4-2
Round 4	West Brom	(h)	1-1
	West Brom	(a)	2-3

1978-79

Round 3	Chelsea	(h)	3-0
Round 4	Fulham	(a)	1-1
	Fulham	(h)	1-0
Round 5	Colchester United	(a)	1-0
Round 6	Spurs	(a)	1-1
	Spurs	(h)	2-0
Semi Final	Liverpool	(Maine Rd)	2-2
	Liverpool	(Goodison)	1-0
Final	Arsenal	(Wembley)	2-3

1979-80

Round 3	Spurs	(a)	1-1
	Spurs	(h)	0-1

1980-81

Round 3	Brighton	(h)	2-2
	Brighton	(a)	2-0
Round 4	Nottingham Forest	(a)	0-1

1981-82

Round 3	Watford	(a)	0-1

1982-83

Round 3	West Ham United	(h)	2-0
Round 4	Luton	(a)	2-0
Round 5	Derby County	(a)	1-0
Round 6	Everton	(h)	1-0
Semi Final	Arsenal	(Villa Park)	2-1
Final	Brighton	(Wembley)	2-2
	Brighton	(Wembley)	4-0

1983-84

Round 3	Bournemouth	(a)	0-2

1984-85

Round 3	Bournemouth	(h)	2-1
Round 4	Coventry	(h)	2-1
Round 5	Blackburn	(a)	2-0
Round 6	West Ham United	(h)	4-2
Semi Final	Liverpool	(Goodison)	2-2
	Liverpool	(Maine Rd)	2-1
Final	Everton	(Wembley)	1-0

1985-86

Round 3	Rochdale	(h)	2-0
Round 4	Sunderland	(a)	0-0
	Sunderland	(h)	3-0
Round 5	West Ham United	(a)	1-1
	West Ham United	(h)	0-2

1986-87

Round 3	Manchester City	(h)	1-0
Round 4	Coventry City	(h)	0-1

1987-88

Round 3	Ipswich Town	(a)	2-1
Round 4	Chelsea	(h)	2-0
Round 5	Arsenal	(a)	1-2

1988-89

Round 3	Queens Park Rangers	(h)	0-0
	Quuens Park Rangers	(a)	2-2
	Queens Park Rangers	(h)	3-0
Round 4	Oxford United	(h)	4-0
Round 5	Bournemouth	(a)	1-1
	Bournemouth	(h)	1-0
Round 6	Nottingham Forest	(h)	0-1

EUROPEAN RECORD

(H° Played at Maine Road, H* Played at Plymouth,
§ After extra time. United scores first)

1956/57 European Cup

Preliminary Round	Anderlecht (Belgium)	12-0	(A 2-0, H° 10-0)
First Round	Borussia Dortmund (West Germany)	3-2	(H° 3-2, A 0-0)
Quarter-Final	Atletico Bilbao (Spain)	6-5	(A 3-5, H° 3-0)
Semi-Final	Real Madrid (Spain)	3-5	(A 1-3, H 2-2)

1957/58 European Cup

Preliminary Round	Shamrock Rovers (Eire)	9-2	(A 6-0, H 3-2)
First Round	Dukla Prague (Czechoslovakia)	3-1	(H 3-0, A 0-1)
Quarter-Final	Red Star Belgrade (Yugoslavia)	5-4	(H 2-1, A 3-3)
Semi-Final	A.C. Milan (Italy)	2-5	(H 2-1, A 0-4)

1963/64 European Cup Winners Cup

First Round	Willem II (Holland)	7-2	(A 1-1, H 6-1)
Second Round	Spurs (England)	4-3	(A 0-2, H 4-1)
Quarter-Final	Sporting Lisbon (Portugal)	4-6	(H 4-1, A 0-5)

1964/65 Inter Cities Fairs Cup

First Round	Djurgardens (Sweden)	7-2	(A 1-1, H 6-1)
Second Round	Borussia Dortmund (West Germany)	10-1	(A 6-1, H 4-0)
Third Round	Everton (England)	3-2	(H 1-1, A 2-1)
Quarter-Final	Racing Strasbourg (France)	5-0	(A 5-0, H 0-0)
Semi-Final	Ferencvaros (Hungary)	4-5	(H 3-2, A 0-1, A 1-2)

1965/66 European Cup

Preliminary Round	J.K. Helsinki (Finland)	9-2	(A 3-2, H 6-0)
First Round	Vorwaerts (East Germany)	5-1	(A 2-0, H 3-1)
Quarter-Final	Benfica (Portugal)	8-3	(H 3-2, A 5-1)
Semi-Final	Partizan Belgrade (Yugoslavia)	1-2	(A 0-2, H 1-0)

1967/68 European Cup

First Round	Hibernians (Malta)	4-0	(H 4-0, A 0-0)
Second Round	A.K. Sarajevo (Yugoslavia)	2-1	(A 0-0, H 2-1)
Quarter-Final	Gornik Zabrze (Poland)	2-1	(H 2-0, A 0-1)
Semi-Final	Real Madrid (Spain)	4-3	(H 1-0, A 3-3)
Final	Benfica (Portugal)	4-1§	(at Wembley)

1968/69 European Cup

First Round	Waterford (Eire)	10-2	(A 3-1, H 7-1)
Second Round	Anderlecht (Belgium)	4-3	(H 3-0, A 1-3)
Quarter-Final	Rapid Vienna (Austria)	3-0	(H 3-0, A 0-0)
Semi-Final	A.C. Milan (Italy)	1-2	(A 0-2, H 1-0)

1976/77 U.E.F.A. Cup

First Round	Ajax (Holland)	2-1	(A 0-1, H 2-0)
Second Round	Juventus (Italy)	1-3	(H 1-0, A 0-3)

1977/78 European Cup Winners Cup

Preliminary Round	St. Etienne (France)	3-1	(A 1-1, H* 2-0)
First Round	F.C. Porto (Portugal)	5-6	(A 0-4, H 5-2)

1980/81 U.E.F.A. Cup

First Round	Widzew Lodz (Poland)	1-1	(H 1-1, A 0-0) Lost on away goals

1982/83 U.E.F.A. Cup

First Round	Valencia (Spain)	1-2	(H 0-0, A 1-2)

1983/84 European Cup Winners Cup

First Round	Dukla Prague (Czechoslovakia)	3-3	(H 1-1, A 2-2) Won on away goals
Second Round	Spartak Varna (Bulgaria)	4-1	(A 2-1, H 2-0)
Quarter-Final	Barcelona (Spain)	3-2	(A 0-2, H 3-0)
Semi-Final	Juventus (Italy)	2-3	(H 1-1, A 1-2)

1984/85 U.E.F.A. Cup

First Round	Raba Gyor (Hungary)	5-2	(H 3-0, A 2-0)
Second Round	Eindhoven (Holland)	1-0	(A 0-0, H 1-0)
Third Round	Dundee United (Scotland)	5-4	(H 2-2, A 3-2)
Fourth Round	Videoton (Hungary)	1-1	(H 1-0, A 0-1) Lost 4-5 on penalties